RESILIE:

STORIES OF RESILIENCE

THIS BOOK BELONGS TO:		
BOOK: THE GLOBAL RESILIENCE PROJECT		

DATE READ	NAME	LOCATION

Created by The Global Resilience Project

Editor: Catherine Nikkel

Book cover design: Ruth Barrow, Whistler Creative whistlercreative.ca

Book design and layout: Ruth Barrow, Whistler Creative whistlercreative.ca

Published by Blair Kaplan Communications, Inc.

blairkaplan.ca

theglobalresilienceproject.com

Disclaimer: Readers of this publication agree that neither Blair Kaplan Venables, Blair Kaplan Communications Inc., Alana Kaplan, Catherine Nikkel, Ruth Barrow, nor The Global Resilience Project will be held responsible or liable for damages that may be alleged or resulting directly or indirectly from the use of this publication. Neither the publisher nor the authors can be held accountable for the information provided or actions resulting from assessing these resources.

Editor's Disclaimer:

As the editorial team, we stand by the integrity and authenticity of the story presented by the author. Every effort has been made to ensure the narrative remains in its truest form, reflecting the author's original intent and voice.

Throughout the editorial process, our commitment has been to preserve the essence and integrity of the author's storytelling. While we have provided guidance and suggestions to enhance clarity and coherence, the core narrative, author preferences, and message remain untouched.

The story you are about to experience represents the genuine expression of the author's vision.

Resilience is the ability to bounce forward from life's most challenging experiences.

We all have the ability to be resilient. We all have a resilience muscle, and we must continuously strengthen it so that when we need to, we can activate it. Life can be hard but know that you are not alone and will get through the dark times.

Dedicated to our beloved Baba Leah, the radiant matriarch of our family, whose warm smile illuminates every corner of our lives.

Your unwavering love, wisdom, and grace have shaped our journey, and this book stands as a tribute to the light you bring into our world. With heartfelt gratitude, we dedicate these pages to you, our guiding star and source of endless inspiration.

"Not choosing life is choosing death."

Leonard Ian Kaplan

November 13, 1955 – February 18, 2022

Note: Upon Blair and Alana's father learning that he was terminally ill with COPD and lung cancer, he made a list of his options. The above quote was the first thing he wrote on that list. Blair found this list almost two years after he passed away.

Foreword

Foreword

In the wake of unexpected challenges, The Global Resilience Project community emerged as a beacon of hope and strength, transforming lives and producing a best-selling book along the way. What began as a personal journey of healing and sharing amidst the turmoil of my father's terminal illness in 2018 has blossomed into a powerful testament to the indomitable human spirit.

As we conclude the second installment of The Global Resilience Project's book series, the evolution of my life since its inception is nothing short of extraordinary. Joined by my sister Alana, we embarked on an important journey, aspiring to create a community of inspiration and resilience for others grappling with their own adversities.

Reflecting on the five-year odyssey, the depth of resilience required has surpassed all expectations. While my father defied the odds and lived longer than anyone thought he would, Alana and I endured the heart-wrenching loss of our mother to a brief battle with cancer. Simultaneously, my husband Shayne faced the tragic passing of his father just three months apart. Amidst these trials, our dad's passing on February 18, 2022, added another layer of profound grief.

He never got to see the finished product of the first book, but we know he is proud of us.

There were moments when doubts clouded my commitment to this project. I questioned its purpose and considered walking away. Yet, amidst the struggle, I rediscovered the essence of resilience – not just moving on, but bouncing forward into something greater and more beautiful after enduring life-altering experiences.

As my understanding of resilience evolved, so did the project's significance. It became a collective force, offering solace and strength to me and everyone touched by its narratives. I realized that taking breaks and seeking rest is as crucial as the relentless pursuit of resilience.

After the first book launched, I wasn't sure if there would be a second. My mother came to me in a dream five months after publishing it. She was there to tell me she was proud of me as I was getting ready to publish our second book. I woke up reinvigorated and inspired and felt like it was time to begin working on this very book that you hold in your hands.

To all who have showered us with love and support over the last half a decade, this book's success is as much yours as it is ours. The resilient humans who shared their stories and the broader community that embraced this journey, your contributions made this achievement possible. You are not alone, and together, we continue to embody the true essence of resilience.

Love,

Blair Kaplan Venables,
Founder of The Global Resilience Project

About the
Authors

Blair Kaplan Venables

Founder,
The Global Resilience Project

Blair Kaplan Venables is a British Columbia-based grief and resilience expert and the Founder of The Global Resilience Project. Her expertise has been featured in media outlets, including Forbes, CBC Radio, Entrepreneur, and Thrive Global. IAOTP named Blair the Top Grief and Resilience Expert of the Year in 2024. USA Today listed Blair as one of the top 10 conscious female leaders to watch, and she empowers others to be resilient from stages around the world. Blair's story of resilience and how The Global Resilience Project came to be will be featured on a new TV show that will be airing on Apple TV+ called 'MyStory.' She is the Radical Resilience podcast's co-host, motivational speaker, and bestselling author. She specializes in helping people strengthen their resilience muscle using scientifically proven methods and supports grievers with her Navigating Grief Framework. In her free time, you can find Blair writing in nature, travelling the world, and helping people through their most challenging moments.

> *"Grief is the afterglow of love's flame."*
>
> – Blair Kaplan Venables

Alana Kaplan

Mental Health Director,
The Global Resilience Project

Alana Kaplan is a compassionate mental health professional based in Winnipeg, Manitoba, Canada. She works in the mental health field in Winnipeg, Manitoba, and is a co-host of the Radical Resilience podcast. Fueled by advocacy, Alana is known for standing up and speaking out for others. Passionate about de-stigmatizing and normalizing mental health, Alana brings her experience to The Global Resilience Project's team, navigating the role one's mental health plays in telling their story.

Engaging in self-care and growth keeps her going, and her love for reading, travel, and personal relationships helps foster that. When she's not working, Alana can often be found on walks, doing a crossword puzzle, or playing with any animal she sees.

> *"The only person you can control is yourself."*
>
> – Alana Kaplan
> (and probably many others)

About This Book

This book aims to help inspire you to be resilient and show you that you are not alone.

RESILIENT A.F.: Stories of Resilience is a collection of stories of resilience from around the world. Telling your story can be a powerful part of your healing journey, and we created a safe space for people to share and read stories of resilience. It's helpful to read other people's stories when going through a tough time because they can inspire you to move through your challenge and feel less alone. Here is what they were asked to do;

- *In one sentence, explain the situation where you had to be resilient.*

- *Please share your story. When you were presented with the situation, What did you feel? How did you react? What went through your mind? How did you cope?*

- *How did you practice resilience when faced with this challenge?*

- *Please share one piece of advice for people who are going through a similar challenge.*

- *We also have some of our coauthors submit their stories by following their creative flow, which we love!*

Resilience
by Alana

Resilience

The Global Resilience Project community defines resilience as the ability to bounce forward from a challenging situation. We don't bounce back to who we were before, as life is not the same as it was in the situation where you had to be resilient. Resilience is a concept that carries a lot of weight, and of course, it goes without saying that life would be easier if we did not have to endure being resilient or working through tough situations.

Unfortunately, especially in 2024, many, if not most of us, have had to overcome and bounce forward from a difficult situation. Whether it is moving through grief, addiction, mental health, war, disability, escaping a toxic relationship/community, or an unpredictable event, resilience is something that connects us all. Whether you live in the prairies in Canada (where I live) or Ghana, the threads sewn throughout the world can connect us all. These connections can evoke many feelings and help you feel validated. That said, you don't have to experience a grandiose life event to identify with resilience. The beauty of resilience is that you can decide for yourself what makes you resilient.

As you read through this book's stories, please pause between each story and reflect. This book isn't meant to be read all in one sitting, and it's important for you to take care of yourself. As a mental health professional on the frontlines in Canada, I am often confronted with stories and experiences laced with resilience. In addition, these experiences are also laced with sadness, hardships, and many other feelings. If I can teach you anything before engaging in this book, it would be to have a self-care plan and boundaries. While it is okay to feel big feelings and experience some emotional dysregulation, put the book down and come back later if you feel like you are no longer in a tolerance zone. Of course, if you need further support, please connect with your local mental health resources, as this book and the lessons shared within it are not a replacement for mental health support. We hope that you take what you need from this book.

Alana Kaplan, Mental Health Director

Table of Contents

Stories of Resiliance:

Introduction + How to use this Book

Unlock your inner resilience—it's a muscle we all possess. Just like any muscle, it thrives when consistently exercised. Strengthen yours now so it's ready to support you when life challenges you .

Empower yourself to navigate tough times with greater ease. A powerful method to fortify your resilience is by sharing your story. Whether in a personal journal, with a trusted therapist, among friends and family, or within our supportive community. The act of sharing has a transformative effect; it aids in your healing process. Moreover, by delving into others' stories contributes to a collective healing experience.

Don't let your experiences stay locked inside. You possess incredible strength and resilience. Let your story be a source of inspiration for yourself and for those who may find solace in your journey. Embrace your resilience—let it shine.

You are strong. You are resilient.

Content Warnings

Within this book are various stories of recovery and resilience beyond trauma. Reading these stories may affect you personally. It may activate a strong emotional response depending on your own experiences. This is entirely normal.

It is important to protect yourself and your energy while engaging with the stories in this book. If you feel activated, pause, put down the book, and take care of yourself. We have put some resources on the next page to support you.

Here are some strategies and resources that may help ground you:

Strategies

5,4,3,2,1 A Sensory Grounding Experience
Name 5 things you can see,
4 things you can feel,
3 things you can hear,
2 things you can smell,
and 1 thing you can taste.

Counting
Count backwards from 100 by 6. By doing this, you are putting your focus on counting and math and taking your mind off the trigger.

Box Breathing
Find a comfortable seat with your feet on the ground. Begin by imagining a square. Using your finger or mind, trace upwards on one side of a square as you inhale for four beats.

Then trace a straight line, left to right, as you hold your breath for another count of 4 beats. Trace down as you exhale for a count of 4. Then trace right to left as you hold your exhale for a count of 4.

Repeat for at least two minutes.

Balloon Breathing
Begin by finding a comfortable seat with your feet on the ground. When you feel safe and comfortable, close your eyes or soften your gaze. Imagine that there is a balloon in front of you. As you inhale, visualize the balloon expanding. As you exhale, visualize the balloon deflating. Repeat 3-5 times at a slow count of 4 beats per breath.

Resources

If you need to talk to someone, here are some numbers that can help:

9-8-8: Suicide Crisis Helpline (Canada)
24/7 Dial 9-8-8 OR Text 9-8-8 or visit 988.ca

Kids Help Phone (Canada)
1-800-668-6868 www.kidshelpphone.ca
An anonymous and confidential phone and text line for children and young adults up to the age of 20.

9-8-8 Suicide and Crisis Lifeline (USA)
24/7 support. Dial 9-8-8 or visit 988lifeline.org

Crisis Text Line UK - Text 'Home' to 85258
Shout - UK'S 24/7 Crisis Text Services
Text 'Shout' to 85258 or visit giveusashout.org

Mental Health Helpline (EU)
Based in Norway, call 116 123 for mental health support.

If you are looking for more resources on mental health, here are some websites:

Canadian Mental Health Association
cmha.ca/ - Located across Canada, CMHA supports and promotes mental health, recovery, and loved ones.

National Alliance on Mental Illness
nami.org/Home - Located in the USA, NAMI is a wealth of mental health resources.

Once you feel like you are grounded, engaging in deep breathing can be helpful to restore your heart rate and focus. With breathing strategies, I recommend breathing through your nose on the inhales and exhales.

Alysha Myronuk

I got married because my father was terminally ill, and then my husband left me 11 months into our marriage, right after we bought the restaurant we met at.

You know the crazy coincidences you can't explain or see the same word or number over and over? I have another name for these signs/synchronicities and coin them as myronies. However, myrony (my+irony) has its own definition of synchronicity in motion. We may see a sign, but then there is an action we can take when we trust that inner knowing, and once we recognize that, we gain a kind of superpower that's in all of us! This is why I am so grateful to tell my story here about not only how resilience plays a key role in facing adversity but also how myrony changed my life once I realized how these incredible signs would appear either before or after following my intuition and I want to show how it can change yours too.

I became aware of myrony almost 20 years ago when my dad became terminally ill, and I ended up getting married at the hospital I was born in, one week before he passed, even though I was not engaged. My then-boyfriend and I had planned on getting married, so after crying to my dad's younger sister at the hospital about how I couldn't believe my dad would not see his only daughter get married, my aunt suggested why don't we so my dad could be there? So, I called him at the restaurant we both worked at, which was called 821.

> ALWAYS trust your intuition and understand your soul has chosen all that has happened, no matter how difficult life has been. This is how we move spiritually from victimhood to resilience and, finally, empowerment!

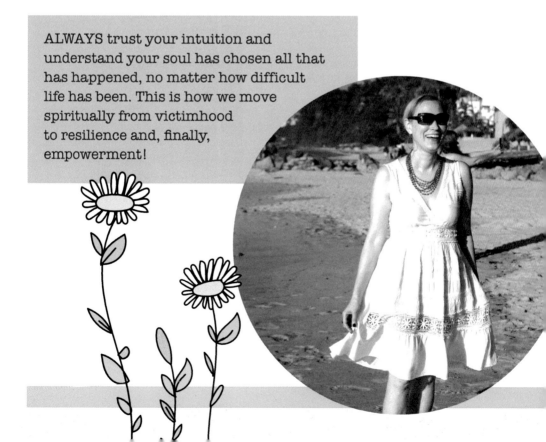

I only mention this because 821 is one of my myronic numbers that showed up repeatedly. It was also here where we met and fell in love, so when I asked if he wanted to get married next Sunday, there was definitely some myrony with me proposing to my future husband at the restaurant we met at while I was in the hospital I was born in. The wedding would also be held in the chapel with the reception outside in the courtyard, so I must be the only one in history born, engaged, and married in the same hospital! The first wedding dress I tried on was the dress of my dreams, and the shoes were the last pair in my size, which truly made me feel like Cinderella. Everything was falling in place until the day before, on August 21st (or 821, which is the restaurant's name, remember?), it was a torrential downpour. Everyone was asking what I would do because the only option was to have the reception in the cafeteria, so I declared, "If there truly is a God, He will not take this away from my father." The next day was one of the most beautiful days I had ever witnessed, with not a drop of rain or a cloud in the sky. That day was so perfect, but I remember later crying hysterically to my new husband since I now knew my dad was going to die; sure enough, exactly one week later, my dad took his last breath with my family around him, and we said goodbye.

Saying goodbye to my dad at the age of 27, I thought, was hard enough; well, I had no idea the crazy twists my life was about to take. After his passing, the owner of 821 asked us to buy it, so we jumped at the opportunity. We were set to purchase on 12/1, but it ended up closing on 12/8, which is 821 reversed, so maybe this was the Universe/God's way of showing me how backward my life was about to get.

My family in May of 2005 then went through another huge loss, which put me in a deeper depression, and that changed my life forever because I ignored every single sign given this one day. A woman who worked for us at the restaurant, during the same time I was dealing with my family's loss, decided she wanted my husband and left hers, and this all started at her son's one-year birthday party. Now, when I say I ignored every sign, including the fact my husband didn't want to go to this party because it was on a Sunday and that was the only day our restaurant was closed. His normal work schedule as Executive Chef was 12-16 hours easily, and I remember him telling me how he just wanted to go home, curl up on our couch with a glass of wine, watch a movie, and just relax. I told him I wished we could do that, but I promised we would go to this party, and then the navigation in our SUV got us so lost we couldn't even find the house for over 45 minutes! What's even worse is I ignored my internal navigation that told me she was up to something, so when he left me 11 months into our marriage, I still had to see him every day because we owned the restaurant, so I'm sure you can imagine my mental state.

My crushing moment was when this woman got pregnant, and I tried to kill myself by drinking a lot of wine, taking a sleeping pill, and then taking a bath. Thankfully, hours later, I woke up in a cold bath, and from then on, I gained barely enough strength to keep going, knowing suicide was not the answer. A few months later, I was given one of the greatest gifts to this day. My friend, who myronically was also my photographer at my wedding, gave me a book that altered my life forever, Many Lives Many Masters by Dr. Brian Weiss. I remember reading how our higher selves choose everything that happens in life. It was so powerful and made me wonder why I would choose this crazy life?!

So from that point on, I would look from that soul perspective, which was how I kept moving forward, and now I believe I chose all the pain and sadness so that I can help others with the incredible tools and insights I discovered along the way. It's actually through the hard times that we later recognize how amazing life is, but thankfully, myrony helps make those difficult times a little easier because the challenges are sometimes the necessary pieces to our life puzzle. If you are intrigued to hear my full myronic story (actually how my last name is pronounced), Ep. 1 of my podcast also explains in much greater depth how EVERYONE experiences these incredible phenomena.

Besides ALWAYS trusting my intuition, the most important thing I learned is how grateful I am and that I have no resentful thoughts. I now look at everything I've been through as a gift, which includes the good, the bad, and especially the ugly. Through the hard times, we later recognize how amazing life is, but thankfully myrony helps make those difficult times a little easier because the challenges are sometimes the necessary pieces to our life puzzle.

I practiced resilience by reading Dr. Brian Weiss's books, of which there are six in total, I have discovered each one holds a key piece to this greater soul awareness, so they actually build upon each other. Something resonated with me that helped me understand that all the pain was part of my life's journey. This kept me going by looking from a higher perspective, and it also helped me let go of all anger/ since, on a soul level, I learned I chose all of this, so I can only blame myself for my crazy myronic life.

ALWAYS trust your intuition and understand your soul has chosen all that has happened, no matter how difficult life has been. This is how we move spiritually from victimhood to resilience and, finally, empowerment!

Alysha Myronuk

Amy Smith -Hightower

An Oreo & Dr. Pepper diet changed my understanding of resilience.

The year was 2017, and I was a devoted Hobby Lobby employee. I was overworked, underpaid, and living on a diet that consisted of my favorite things: Oreos and Dr. Pepper.

> I have also learned that the purpose of food is to fuel our bodies and to do this with the dedication we deserve to ensure optimal long-term health.

Like many Americans, my husband and I lived paycheck to paycheck, surviving off increasingly absurd credit card balances when he was laid off. The only solution I could think of was to work more and spend less. And… like many Americans, my health began to plummet at the age of 36. Imagine, I was 36 years old, and the doctors were telling me my blood pressure was dangerously high, my fluctuating weight was out of control, my blood sugar was pre-diabetic, and the insurance copay was $500 a month (this was just medications let alone the cost of medical bills).

Afraid, broke, and feeling hopeless, the only thing I could do was to deep-dive into ways I could get my health under control because although Oreos and Dr. Pepper were cheap and delicious, these choices were costing me my health. My first attempt at learning how to fuel my body regeneratively was a flop - a lifetime of poor eating habits had left me struggling to figure out what others made look so easy! Unable to hire a dietician or health coach, I began a journey that I couldn't begin to imagine the outcome of.

I tried many of the popular diets. One's that were severely restrictive, others required a lot more cooking than I had time for, and others were just downright unhealthy despite the pounds being shed. All of this until I discovered the single lifestyle change that would alter my life and the lives of tens of thousands of Americans.

I began documenting my simple lifestyle changes on Facebook, including all the times I failed and had to start again from scratch. I was determined to develop the most straightforward ways to achieve better health. I made more mistakes than I can remember, and I had so many small incremental successes. What came next was unimaginable.

I had inadvertently started a community for people just like me. People who were struggling to stay alive. People who were not the greatest in the kitchen but wanted to try simple new recipes. People who didn't have the time or longevity to make all the same mistakes I had.

This was exactly what I needed and what tens of thousands of others needed as well. We encouraged each other; we shared wins and losses, shared personal endeavors, and grew together as a community. This community created accountability for myself that I would have never gotten from anywhere else. I had a sense of purpose and was determined to develop a safe place for us all to land.

It didn't stop at sharing recipes, healthier alternatives to what we were used to, and virtual high fives. Once my weight and the rest of my health were under control, I discovered that our struggles with food stemmed from places much deeper than our pantries.

We were all real people with real emotions; to remain healthy and healing, we needed more. I decided to do more for my mental wellness and to share this as well. Prayer, journaling, fitness (okay, walks), hydration, clean(er) household products, and healthier people in our circles are all aspects of our journey's that we share.

Ultimately, I am not the fanciest cook. I'm not techy when it comes to social media. I am not highly educated in how our bodies work. I'm not trying to impress anyone. I wholeheartedly want as many people as possible to be able to rescue themselves with the simplest, most effective methods that require little to no understanding of biology or at an extra cost. I genuinely believe that being healthier should not be out of anyone's reach.

What started as a way to share who I am and to hold myself accountable has turned into a Facebook community of over 190 thousand people and a business with hundreds of (very uncomfortable in the beginning) videos and meal plans that when I first started creating them for my community, I wrote them out on note cards using a pack I picked up from the Dollar Tree. Tons of recipes, tips, tricks, shopping ideas, money-saving secrets, mistakes (and recoveries), tried and accurate Amazon shopping lists, blogs, community recipe shares, links to products that work, general information, and community discussions.

Even as I have gone through some recent health scares, it is this community that keeps me focused on something greater than myself.

It would be overly simplified to say I have permanently given up Oreos and Dr. Pepper and replaced them with simple but incredibly delicious meals. I have given up familiar foods and snacks that, at the time, served a purpose. I have also learned that the purpose of food is to fuel our bodies and to do this with the dedication we deserve to ensure optimal long-term health. I have given up the old Amy and created space for the new and improved Amy. I have maintained a healthy weight for many years, but this is not the only purpose of my changes. My blood pressure is normal, my blood sugar is normal, and I no longer require medications to keep me alive. Albeit long-term stress and a poor diet have certainly contributed to some more recent health hiccups, but I feel like a different person.

In turn, I have discovered an entire community of people who want to live their best lives so we can show others it can be done with support, love, and acceptance. We want to leave the world a little brighter. And we want to do this with grace and resilience because we all deserve to live the healthiest versions of ourselves - simply.

This story of resilience belongs to all of us.

Amy Smith-Hightower

Amy Thurman

After passing out unexpectedly, only months later, did I learn what actually had happened. I had broken my neck.

Startled awake during the night by an intense pain in my abdomen, I remember hearing the crisp spring wind blowing outside in April 2014. As I clumsily stumbled in the dark toward the medicine cabinet in search of relief, the pain began to sharpen, accompanied by an intense bout of dizziness and nausea.

Folding in half like a book meeting itself when it's closed, my body could no longer hold itself upright as the nausea intensified, and the dizziness caused the room to spin and my vision to turn black. I ended up in a ball against the wall on the hardwood floor with zero ideas of what to do.

Always the independent one who ignored limits and refused to listen to the voice of reason, calling out for help never crossed my mind. I was determined to take myself back to bed and began mentally psyching myself up to stand upright again.

Holding onto the wall for stability, I reached my feet and took two steps toward my bed. That's the last thing I remember before I awoke in a heap on my face on the other side of the house on the living room floor.

The impact from inadvertently slamming my face onto the hardwood floor sheared my brain stem and caused a traumatic brain injury and a broken neck that went undetected for six months. My doctor would later tell me that the fact that I survived was a miracle.

I had been the mom who shuttled her kids around everywhere, volunteered every weekend, and worked an insane number of hours at her full-time job. I didn't have time for any type of injury, much less one of this caliber.

Instead of being able to take care of everyone as I had been accustomed to, I could no longer take care of myself and would be confined to bed, forced to lay flat for 23 hours a day for the following year. Walking, talking, hearing or seeing correctly, and taking myself to the restroom were no longer things I could do.

As you can imagine, I went into a deep, dark place that I would never wish on anyone. Completely missing a year of my children's lives, I felt they would be better off without the burden that I was, so I began praying that I would die and developed a plan to use my pain medicine to make it happen.

As my plan was unfolding, in a brief moment of clarity, I remember thinking, "What if dying is not the answer? What if instead of fighting so hard to die, I fight to live? Maybe my experience can help someone else if I can get better."

If I could leave you with one piece of advice the next time you are faced with a challenge, it would be that instead of listening to the voice in your head telling you what's impossible, open yourself to the messages your soul longs to share with you about what is possible.

As a former educator and social worker, that's when my story took a turn. I began fighting to live with the intention of using my story to help others.

This brought with it an intense desire to replace the negativity that was living in my head and heart with something, anything, that would help me get out of that prison cell that resembled my bed.

Pouring over teachings from Tony Robbins, Dr. Wayne Dyer, Rumi, and other luminaries caused a shift in my perspective that became the catalyst I needed to propel me forward, defying the limitations imposed upon me. I reclaimed my life, refusing to be a victim of circumstance, and that's when my business, Polish the Mirror, was born.

Named after this poem by Rumi, Polish the Mirror is a philosophy that embodies the essence of finding the answers we seek by looking within.

"Ye who seek God, apart;
That which you seek, thou art.
If you wish to seek the Beloved's face,
Polish the mirror and gaze into that space."

Losing everything that defined my worth became an opportunity for reinvention, an unwavering pursuit of rewriting my own story.

I'm Amy Thurman, and I have lived the past ten years with a broken neck.

My resilience journey is a testament to the incredible strength we all have within us. I changed my mindset and started fighting to live instead of fighting to die.

If I could leave you with one piece of advice the next time you are faced with a challenge, it would be that instead of listening to the voice in your head telling you what's impossible, open yourself to the messages your soul longs to share with you about what is possible.

Thank you for reading my story of triumph and the relentless pursuit of a new beginning.

Amy Thurman

Andrea Smith

After my divorce, I embarked on a journey of rebuilding my life, navigating through the challenges of starting a new job, establishing a new home, and rediscovering my identity as an individual; it demanded time, reflection, conversations with God, and faith, yet within that safe space, I not only persevered but emerged on the other side thriving.

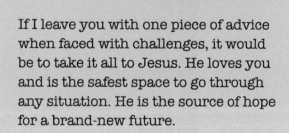

If I leave you with one piece of advice when faced with challenges, it would be to take it all to Jesus. He loves you and is the safest space to go through any situation. He is the source of hope for a brand-new future.

In 2018, my marriage ended, and I started over. It was a time of dealing with being rejected and struggling with self-worth, but also a sense of relief that I was now finally removed from the situation. Over time, in order to adapt and keep the peace, and for fear of having my needs go unmet, I became a shell of who I was.

After it was over and now going through some major changes (moving and a new job within two weeks), what really helped me regroup was having my own place as a safe space to allow God to remind me who I was, a steady job that I enjoyed and paid enough for me to live on my own and having a community of good friends nearby who could be that listening ear, sounding board and those people who could speak life back into my life. It was a period of relearning to see and love myself for who I was. It was a time of learning that I am loved and enough because God says so, and nothing matters more than that. I have been a people pleaser for years, having the idea constantly reaffirmed that love is conditional based on what I do and what I can produce.

I have believed for years that I have been both too much and not enough at the same time for people, making it hard to not only express my own needs but also meet the needs of others. Slowly, over the years, I have also learned that external validation is not where my worth comes from, although it is easy to fall back into that way of thinking sometimes. This new beginning also put me in a position where I couldn't rely on someone else to support me, whether financially or emotionally. It allowed me to see what I was capable of and deepen my relationship with Jesus. He showed up for me in people, in my personal devotions, in circumstances that could not be humanly organized, and led me into a brighter, hopeful future. As I rebuilt my life over the course of 5 years, I could once again look past myself and have characteristics like serving, leadership, and loving people through outreach and relationships come back to life.

I started my own charity in 2021, focusing on poverty reduction and human trafficking prevention. That has always been a major life goal for me.

I found my place in my church through involvement with youth and leadership. I started volunteering again and doing the things that I loved. I am not totally healed from my feelings of being rejected or insecurity at not being enough, but healing is a process, and it's something that I need to work on every day. And it's not all intense. For me, healing has included learning what it means to have fun again and putting myself back out there. I'm learning to love the process, the daily activities, and the life that I am working on building.

I know that I wouldn't be where I am today if I had chosen to give up before or at any point in my life when things have unraveled. I have learned to actively look for the good even when things are less than ideal.

Throughout my story, I practiced resilience by digging deeper into my faith and relationship with Jesus, self-care, consistent and stable work, building a community of people who could love and support me through my healing journey, and doing things I loved.

If I leave you with one piece of advice when faced with challenges, it would be to take it all to Jesus. He loves you and is the safest space to go through any situation. He is the source of hope for a brand-new future.

Andrea Smith

Barbie Layton

I had a near-death experience with almost always fatal E. coli in 2012 and realized that resilience and gratitude were all that was left.

Resilience is a beautiful concept, an unwavering beacon of hope that speaks to the heart of every human being. It's the ability to bounce back from life's most challenging moments, recover from adversity, and emerge stronger and wiser. It's like a magical elixir flowing through the world's veins. It's what keeps us standing when the storms of life threaten to knock us down. Resilience can be a kind of North Star. It's the guiding light that leads us through the darkest of times.

When practicing resilience, I went into trusting in my faith, practicing gratitude, and keeping hope alive.

In 2012, I was at work, and my coworkers told me I was pale as a ghost and hot and cold all day. I had no idea how close to the end I was! I had just changed insurance, and my policy didn't start until the 1st of October, so I waited. I saw the doctor, and she told me it was nothing; then, the next day, I ended up in the emergency room and was rushed to a CAT scan machine. The radiologist surgically aspirated 55 cc of what they later identified as E. coli out of a pearl-shaped fluid sac that had grown in my abdomen and showed me the toxic green-colored fluid!

They had to send the sample through the CDC to verify as they'd never seen anything like it! The doctor thought my international travels probably contributed to it over the years. I was in and out of consciousness for almost three weeks, my hair turned white from severe oxidative stress, and they had to do four more aspiration surgeries that were very painful. I was very scared that I wouldn't make it, and I was on the highest level of antibiotics that wreaked havoc in my body. It was a brand new hospital, and I was in a suite on the 5th floor with a wide picture window overlooking the freeway and the mountains and sky in Southern California. I spent a lot of time looking out of that window and wondering if life would ever be the same or if I would make it.

During that time, they kept telling me I had an incurable illness that I didn't want to face even though the symptoms were there. But, having previously bounced back from multiple near-death experiences that were not related, I made the decision that I would beat this. Resilience is often deciding and overcoming challenges despite the odds, feeling like they're against you. The power of resilience lies not just in bouncing back but in adapting and evolving. Sometimes, it's needed to go through a difficult or painful situation, as I see it as a muscle.

The beautiful emperor butterfly goes through a painful chrysalis, and scientists did an experiment to make it less painful so they cut open a side to let it out more easily. When it came out, it was deformed and couldn't fly. The chrysalis, while painful and uncertain, is necessary. Those kinds of shortcuts don't allow us to grow and see the inner strength that we're made of. When we have the muscle of resilience, it helps us to be beautifully broken open, and it is often the beginning of a journey or a personal quest, kind of like Bilbo Baggins in "The Lord of the Rings," who has to leave the Shire.

Until you have to adapt and shift your perspective when you are pushed out of your comfort zone, you don't actually know what you're capable of. Not all coping mechanisms are healthy, and I definitely knew I couldn't do a spiritual bypass and pretend everything was fine. It's not all unicorns and rainbows, and I had to honor my pain and healing journey that I'm still on right now. It's been a marathon, not a sprint.

A lot of my coping was around fashion therapy and dressing for success to upgrade my mood. That brought some joy into an otherwise dismal experience and helped bring mindfulness into the moment. If I'm feeling low, wearing sweats and no makeup is the worst thing I can do, as it exacerbates it. When I get dressed up, I feel better and bring my best self, even if I'm not feeling well, and the energy of play and childlike wonder comes through, a vibration the universe loves! Nikola Tesla said the world is made up of energy, vibration, and frequency.

When I am not feeling well, I focus on extreme gratitude for the journey and all the things I have as opposed to what I do not. Coming back into the center of your heartbeat, your breathing, saying thank you for the chair you're sitting on, the food that is available to you, the electricity you have, the water that is flowing through your pipes, when you get to gratitude stacking over 15 things, you realize that you are supported by so many unseen people who are keeping the structure of your life intact.

As I've journeyed through this world, I've learned that kindness and resilience go hand in hand. The more we cultivate resilience in our lives, the more kindness we can spread. When we help others bounce back from adversity, we contribute to a more compassionate world. We have the opportunity to leave a legacy for generations to come.

As I've discovered on my journey of personal growth and overcoming adversities, there's no greater gift we can give ourselves and our world than resilience in the form of determination and perseverance. In its embrace, we find the power to heal, transform, and, ultimately, create a more compassionate and united global community. By sharing our personal stories, we can inspire and write new chapters in the story of our lives, and kindness is the song we sing.

When practicing resilience, I went into trusting in my faith, practicing gratitude, and keeping hope alive.

A final note: I remember in 2021, driving to a media coaching event in Scottsdale, Arizona, on the freeway by the hospital I had stayed in and seeing my room and crying that I was moving into a new stage of my life and thanking my soul, my body, and the divine for keeping me alive so I could inspire others with my story.

And for you, I hope you never give up, lean into your inner reserves of strength, and stay focused on your untapped resilience.

Barbie Layton

Blair Kaplan Venables

I walked away from a high-paying client due to antisemitism right at the beginning of the pandemic, as the world was shutting down.

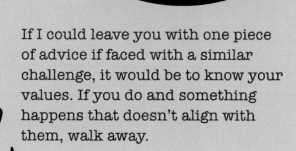

If I could leave you with one piece of advice if faced with a similar challenge, it would be to know your values. If you do and something happens that doesn't align with them, walk away.

As a proud Jewish woman, I always believed I'd be shielded from the harsh reality of blatant antisemitism. Yet, there I was, facing it head-on and feeling isolated when I reached out for support.

From my earliest days at Hebrew school, I was immersed in the stories of our past, from the Holocaust to World War II, absorbing the resilience of my people. Anne Frank's story, in particular, left a lasting impression on me, instilling a deep sense of vigilance. It may sound extreme, but I grew up with a keen awareness of where to hide should the unthinkable ever happen. This level of caution, I've found, isn't uncommon among us.

Living in a predominantly Jewish neighborhood and attending Hebrew school insulated me from overt antisemitism. At most, I encountered stereotypes, which I didn't hesitate to correct and educate on. But growing up, I did face subtle microaggressions and comments about "looking Jewish" that hinted at deeper prejudices. Note: I am of Eastern European descent, and you can't "look" like a religion.

My career eventually took me to a beautiful mountain town in British Columbia, where I worked with a diverse, highly educated team helping clients launch their brands. It was a far cry from my sheltered upbringing, exposing me to a broader world yet also to its underlying biases.

A more recent incident shook me deeply. A colleague, under the guise of humor, made offensive jokes and comments about Jews. I tried to address it through education, hoping for understanding. However, the situation escalated when, during a discussion about a work trip to Germany, this person directed a "Hail Hitler" salute at me, laughing it off as a joke. The silence from everyone else was deafening.

With Holocaust Memorial Day looming, the gesture cut deeper, a stark reminder of the pain and suffering endured by my ancestors. I reported the incident, only to be met with gaslighting from my supervisor, who trivialized the antisemitism and made me feel like the problem. Deep down in my core, I knew that the colleague was in the wrong.

The lack of support and accountability left me feeling unsafe. I had to make a tough decision for my mental health and safety, choosing to leave behind a toxic environment where my concerns were dismissed and I wasn't protected. This was a scary time because the world was on the brink of pandemic lockdowns, and my financial situation was precarious, but I had to do the right thing. Though I sought legal advice, prioritizing my well-being meant walking away from a situation where I was blatantly disrespected and invalidated.

When faced with the need for resilience, I listened to my gut and knew what happened wasn't right. I stood up for what I believed in and had faith that the universe would help take care of me.

If I could leave you with one piece of advice if faced with a similar challenge, it would be to know your values. If you do and something happens that doesn't align with them, walk away.

Blair Kaplan Venables

Charlese Latham

I had an emergency back injury that rendered me unable to walk.

I'm no stranger to hard times. At the age of 6, I was savagely bit in the face by my friend's dog during a backyard BBQ. It took weeks in the hospital, years of surgeries, and my entire life before I overcame the trauma and embarrassment that come with facial scars and almost losing sight during a tussle with a pit bull. The feelings continued into my teen years, which were difficult for reasons I didn't understand.

I never felt like I fit in and couldn't decide if I wanted to. It was the 90s; it was cool to be an outlier. It was also undiagnosed clinical depression. Yet, I worked hard at school and graduated earlier than my friends to find my way. I took my first job as soon as my permit allowed and felt like an adult years before my friends. I enjoyed being an overachiever.

As an adult, I kept to the same habit of working hard and throwing myself into solutions when times got difficult. It always felt best to do everything I possibly could in the face of scary times. Perhaps the harder I tried, the more control I would have, right?

While that often worked, it took its toll on my physical and mental health. When my marriage got tough, financial issues reared their ugly heads, and I was in multiple car accidents, I just did everything necessary to keep going. When I hated the salon I worked in, I designed, built, and opened my own. I always believed I could do anything I put my mind to.

It was hard to ignore the physical toll my career and circumstances took on my body. Week after week, I felt more pain as I juggled my clients and their needs. I would stretch, take copious amounts of Advil, and use the wall to lean on so it wasn't apparent to anyone else how bad it was getting. I thought it was working, and I was fooling myself. I kept on like this… until I couldn't.

One day in December of 2018, I awoke to a new problem. My biggest one yet. I couldn't walk. I called friends to help me use the restroom, walk my dog, and take me to Urgent Care. But it wasn't a temporary setback. This was a life-changing development.

Within three weeks, I was forced to call 9-11 and enter the Emergency Room. My spinal disc between L4 and L5 had exploded and pinched off nerves on the side of my spine, the very ones I needed to feel my toes and move my feet. I needed surgery.

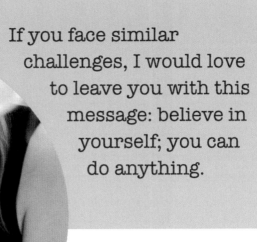

> If you face similar challenges, I would love to leave you with this message: believe in yourself; you can do anything.

But the ER didn't want me to stay. They tried three times to put me in an Über despite being unable to hold myself upright. By 2 am, they had pumped me full of morphine and other pain meds– I was telling stories and laughing about who-knows-what?– and was told I was good enough to go home.

Through pain and grogginess from the meds, I fought for my health and my life. I dug up that old scrappiness and put it to work. It took three days of arguing with doctors (and excruciating pain!) before a neurologist agreed to fix my back and keep me from becoming permanently paralyzed.

The surgery was a success, even though it all led to changing my career and living location.

In this fight for my life, I was more alone than ever. My belief in myself and my desire to find relief fueled my fight and became the strength I needed. When it seemed like giving up was easier, I knew pushing through and demanding what was right would be the only way to survive. I had practiced it before, so it became easier this time. And when I experience difficult times again, I always know how to face them – with less fear than ever.

When faced with this challenge, I relied on practiced courage and stood up for myself as always. There were doctors for weeks telling me I didn't need surgery. Just take the time to relax and let the pain meds help. As nerve damage spread to my toes and ankle, I feared I would lose the ability to walk at all if I let this go on. Through morphine-induced fatigue, I ask doctors, nurses, and eventually my case worker for help. And finally, a neurosurgeon's assistant listened to my story and came to my rescue. After three weeks of fighting for my health and three days in the hospital, I finally was given the procedure I needed all along.

If you face similar challenges, I would love to leave you with this message: believe in yourself; you can do anything.

Charlese Latham

Crystal Adair-Benning

Girlhood dreams don't always go according to plan... even if you are the world's best wedding planner, writer, or... whatever.

A sucker punch to the gut. The wind rushed from my ribcage, expelling out my cheeks faster than the car could slow.

"What happened?" echoes in my ears as my husband maneuvered our rental car across a dangerously narrow strip of pavement onto a side street marked DO NOT ENTER in angry red caps.

We stop, and I try to find my breath. It's as if the pavement under our car is swallowing me whole. I'm beginning to see stars; the multicolored floral lupin blooms are spinning before my eyes.

"I didn't get the Visa. They won't let me on the flight. I'm stuck in Melbourne," I hear our award-winning photographer express in a rapid outburst to my husband.

"I won't be there. I can't make it. She [meaning the Flight Attendant] won't let me on the flight. I don't know what to do."

It's my worst nightmare. Okay, our worst nightmare.

My husband has meticulously been planning this dream wedding for me for no less than four and a half years, ever since my vision of the perfect wedding was expressed over a glass of 2016 Two Sisters Vineyards Reisling and a daydreamy far-off stare caught him straight in the heartstrings.

Now, we've been married no less than eight times before. Yes, eight.

There was our original elopement. The unicorn vow renewal for family. A Shaman in Mexico. Naked underwater in Fiji. Rainstorm in the Scottish highlands. Playful summer heatwave vows in Bath, England—late-night party shenanigans in Croatia. And yes, New Zealand even had a vow renewal atop The Remarkables.

But, it was never THE wedding. The one I'd been dreaming of since the idea of meeting my person and getting married ever formed in my over-Disney'd brain. You know, the wedding you dream of, think of, fantasize about… this was that wedding.

> Just breathe. A 'dream shift' isn't a 'dream death.' It's a moment to pause, reconsider, and reflect... then ask for help. Always look for the Helpers. If you're lucky, you'll marry one.

And now, with a phone call, it wasn't happening.

I was crushed.

Okay, backstory time. I had been a luxury wedding planner for over two decades, planning romantic dream celebrations for couples madly in love since I was in my 20s. I'd travelled the world following love, celebrating love. I'd been married and divorced, and only four and a half years ago… married again. To a dimples-for-days-dude, I met and married in only a month.

When you know, you know. I knew.

But on this hot summer day, along a mountain cross in New Zealand, feeling the dream slip through my fingers, I felt the crush of disappointment worse than the day the doctors told me I had cancer or even the time I ended up in Palliative Care with pancreatitis. This wasn't facing death. This was a total dream disappointment. I had made peace with death in my 20s when it knocked and again in my 30s.

The only dream I had both times was…
this elopement
this dress
this day
this moment
this memory.

And now, while I would not die from a missed wedding, I would face the disappointment of a dream unrealized.

I shook my head at my husband as I wiped back the tears. Big girl panties and all, right, babes? I've got this. I've been disappointed before. My wedding dress (the only true wedding dress I've had with any of our weddings) also didn't make it. It was rumoured and confirmed the dress designer was going out of business. The dress hadn't arrived. The vision was already tarnished.

I stabilize my voice and hear myself say, "It's okay. These things happen. Guess this dream was just too big." A little piece of my soul wavers and withers.

It's true. It's just a wedding. Another in a grand lineup of weddings. It may be the wedding, but it's just a day, a moment, a memory. If not now… sometime later, right?

I mean, sure, the lupins won't be in bloom, and the weather may not be as spectacular as it is right now. Sure, our friends won't be there, and maybe the dress will be different. The dream will have to shift, but it's doable… right?

My heart sinks for the childhood fantasy that's kept me going this long - through health scares and breakups, bankruptcies, and business shifts.

The car whirls around and heads into town. We park up at a spot across from the water, and I stare off into the abyss of glittering sunbeams bouncing off the water. "Maybe some dreams aren't meant to come true," I hear myself saying out loud.

"I promise you, one day, this will happen. I will give you your dream wedding," my husband mutters into my freshly washed chestnut brown hair. "Someday."

"Maybe it's time to give up the dream, babe."

"Never."

We opt instead to renew our vows with friends on the ground in a closet-found dress, a plastered smile, and a sense of adventure. Wedding number nine was filled with so much love.

Sixteen days later, on a perfect summer day, wearing the dress of my dreams and holding my husband's hand, our photographer met us at the airport. "Let's do this," she exclaimed. We clamour into the backseat of a jet-black helicopter and head up, up, up into the mountains, landing deep in a hidden pass accessible only via rugged hikers brave enough to venture here… and us. We climb over mountains and scurry along valley trails. We end up, just us, on Roy's Peak at sunset, whispering vows to each other that are forever etched on my soul.

He found the dress. He got it here. It fits like a glove. He organized the photographer's Visa and got her on another flight. He changed our heli schedule. He ordered a stunning bouquet. He made the dream a reality.

It took two decades, some cracked dreams, and a husband who wouldn't back down from a challenge to make my childhood dream come true. The dream needed help. I married a Helper. Turns out the dream wasn't a wedding… it was a partner that would help make my wildest dreams come true.

Resilience is a drive. A passion for overcoming obstacles, finding new pathways, and finding help along the way. May you find your own Resilience Drive, too.

Just breathe. A 'dream shift' isn't a 'dream death.' It's a moment to pause, reconsider, and reflect… then ask for help. Always look for the Helpers. If you're lucky, you'll marry one.

If I could leave you with a piece of advice when faced with resilience, it would be to choose faith over fear—interest instead of outrage. Resilience is holding the vision so strongly in your heart that even if it does not happen as expected, it doesn't mean it won't happen… eventually. Faith is knowing that it will unfold exactly as it should. Always.

Crystal Adair-Benning

Curtis Shewell

When my oldest daughter was diagnosed with cancer involving multiple tumors in her brain, our lives turned upside down literally in a day.

I practiced resilience by embracing empathy, prioritizing others over myself, adapting to challenges, and having faith in the future. My family and I continued to push forward no matter what was thrown at us, which led me to my miracle job, which changed my life and allowed me to change other lives daily.

After resigning from my job to try to find a miracle cure for her, we no longer had income, which caused a lot of financial issues, and I still had four other children that I had to take care of, including one in college. We had to fight relentlessly to keep things on track at home for the other children and try to figure out how to keep a roof over our heads.

In the face of my daughter's aggressive cancer diagnosis, a flood of emotions rushed in: fear, sorrow, the weight of an uncertain future, the feeling of helplessness, the mental state of knowing you can't protect your child from what's happening. When you only have one job, protect and care for them. All these emotions help you look deep within yourself to figure out how to stay resilient, focused, and positive in the face of the worst adversity you can imagine.

Navigating through the three-year journey, I found strength in Stephanie's astounding resilience within herself and the infectious joy she provided everyone, transforming that pain into a catalyst for personal growth. When I resigned from my job, which required me to travel out of state regularly, I didn't think twice about making that decision even though it would put us in a very difficult spot financially. Yes, the bills stacked up. Yes, we became quickly behind and faced the potential loss of our home, cars, and everything we deemed normal. The financial struggles are real, but they become secondary to the task at hand.

Never giving up hope, never taking our eye off what the challenges were after repeated surgeries, watching this beautiful eight-year-old fight through each of these battles on her own became a pivotal moment. This is when I learned to stop and smell the roses. I realized the biggest doors swing on the smallest hinges and see the light in the darkest moments.

There was a knock at the door, and these two gentlemen were standing there, declaring they were from a local charity and they were trying to figure out a way to help us. The charities are terrific, and usually, the best they can do is provide some sort of financial assistance. After sitting with them for over an hour, going through the stacks of bills and everything financially overwhelming, they asked if they could pay a few of the bills. We all joked, looking at the daunting task of seeing where progress could barely be made at this point.

At the end of the day, we all agreed that no matter which bill or two they could assist with, nothing would change the inevitable. What I really needed was a miracle job. I was not above a handout, but it would not change anything. They asked me what a miracle job looked like, and I explained to them I knew how to sell. It didn't matter the product; I knew I could sell anything, but I needed a job that would allow me to be paid commissions, have an extremely flexible schedule, and be able to leave at a phone calls notice to go to Children's Hospital or Saint Jude, or several other facilities that we had been engaged with. I told them that while I was gone, someone needed to work and close my deals, pay me, and welcome me with open arms whenever I returned. I told them if they could find me a miracle job, I would be indebted to them for life.

The next day, one of the gentlemen called me and asked me if I could take a phone call. I said yes, and a moment later, his son called me. His son was the Vice President of Sales for one of the largest builders in the country. We happened to live in one of the homes that they built. After speaking with him for a minute or two, he said he would like me to work for him. I told him I wasn't very good with a hammer, so what did he have in mind? He laughed and said I want you to come and sell homes for me. You live in one of our homes; you've experienced our process, and we would like you to represent us in selling the same home you live in in our new subdivision.

I started the next day. He set up compensation for me to be paid for selling homes while giving me all the flexibility, freedom, and ability to prioritize my family without compromising.

It's been 16 years since Stephanie went to heaven, yet my miracle job remains. I now have the ability to help so many families and agents across the country. I run one of the largest teams in Michigan. I mentor, train, and coach over 3400 agents within our brokerage at eXp Realty. My miracle job allowed me to help people in ways I never thought possible.

I practiced resilience by embracing empathy, prioritizing others over myself, adapting to challenges, and having faith in the future. My family and I continued to push forward no matter what was thrown at us, which led me to my miracle job, which changed my life and allowed me to change other lives daily.

Curtis Shewell

Deb Drummond

I never saw it coming ...

As I sit here reflecting, wondering about all the times in my life when I had to lean into my inner core and hold on for dear life (what some people call resistance), it makes me feel two things.

My career is talking to women and men daily with dreams and aspirations in their businesses and personal lives.

It has done two things for me: it made me realize my trauma is not singular and how there really is no choice but to get through those things in life that can damage your soul.

I would be lying if I said I wasn't nervous about sharing my trauma or recovery from it in a book with pages to be read by anyone at any time.

Before I had children, I was much more apt to share wherever I was called to share if my story could help another.

It took many years of therapy to recover from some of the things in my life. As many traumas create the same feelings like shame, lack of trust, inability to stand up for oneself, or flashbacks of times in weakness or pain, it can be hard to decipher what experiences I was having in the now were due to what experience I had in the past.

I've been on the planet long enough to know most challenges, the big ones anyway can run deep into childhood wounds or at least trigger them.

Even today, as strong as I am and as happy with my life and the legacy I have built, I am human and have "those moments " when I question my self-esteem and find myself saying yes when I want to say no or no reason what so ever can't get a sense of my accomplishments and be proud of myself.

These might be similar to all people. I know my conversations with many other people express they can have similar experiences, but when sharing with other trauma survivors, the similar triggers make themselves known.

My years away from the actual incidents have been a time where I have gained great strength and wisdom over the results of such experiences.

Many years with a trusted therapist, classes, courses, books, speakers, groups, and other healers and healing sessions have helped me heal the wound and allowed me to stand up in my life in a way I never foresaw.

> Just keep working on you. Keep loving you. Don't let it take your kindness. Don't let it take you hope. And my dear sister or brother survivor….Love, love, love, love yourself.

One day, I will write the whole story, but when Blair asked me to be a part of this project, the downloading I got from my divine self was that someone needed to hear that they too can recover from domestic violence like I have and not only recover but build a life of dreams and choices that you never ever thought was possible.

I want to make a notice here as I am publicly known, as well as my family, that the domestic violence I share in this book was not by the fathers of my children.

Violence was not unknown to me before I experienced it from a partner.

I know domestic violence doesn't have any prerequisites; it can happen to anyone in any situation, but for me, it was part of my life from an early age.

I remember being 5, maybe 6, and making a clear decision in my head that my life would be completely different on many levels.

I can tell you to this day. I remember standing outside on the sidewalk looking at my home, and I said I'm out of here, and my life will never be like this life again.

Today, I can say that is true.

The road to get here has had its brambles, and one of those was my experience with violence in my love relationships.

I can say I know real fear over if I stayed, and my life would definitely be over if I left.

I remember thinking staying was actually my way of staying alive.

I remember being at work and my partner coming in and cornering me for hours at my place of work. I stood in a corner with my partner blocking me from leaving, and everyone else being just too scared to help.

I remember jumping out of the top window of a three-story home, thinking if I broke my leg jumping, at least I would still be alive.

I remember a whole bunch of friends camping on a very high cliff, on a mountain, and no one saw him push me off that cliff in the middle of the night. It took me 4 hours in the dark and in a lot of pain to climb back up to the cliff with every rib broken.

I had to pretend to everyone that I had fallen.

I remember escaping and calling the police to drive me to a safe place and the officer trying to get me to see that there was a better way to live.

I just couldn't see it. My life just never had a strong enough experience or memory bank full of "safe" to know what that officer was talking about. I couldn't relate, so I never saw my own way out.

I also remember being so ashamed that I covered up the stories for him, never made him at fault to other people if anyone knew at all.

I just pretended it didn't happen. Those that did know, I don't think, really knew what to do.

Many of "our" friends, I think, were scared to say anything in case the violence went in their direction.

I lived a quiet, painful existence and didn't feel safe enough anywhere to go, so I stayed.

There wasn't the information widely shared like today about others having this experience.

Like many survivors, the time came when the last hit was the last hit.

One day, for no other days reason other than the voice of his mother…

A month or so before I left him, she and I were home alone one night and had a few glasses of wine, which she never did, and she looked me straight in the eye and said you are too good for my son. I looked at her and knew she knew things I didn't, and she meant it, and I FELT it.

My fight inside to live overrode my fear of dying. I think my soul was on its last piece of sanity, and I thought I would rather die staying or die leaving, and dying trying to leave felt like the only choice I had.

I found an excuse and held onto it like never before. I found out he had an affair, and so it gave me a justified reason in his mind (important when you are trying to leave someone who doesn't allow you to have a voice)

Leaving wasn't easy. He didn't make it easy; it was haunting, and I didn't know if I would make it out. I had to withstand a lot of emotional turmoil, fear, and unknownness, but one day I was free.

Domestic violence was a part of my life for a time, and I seemed not to be able to see the signs. The partners I chose were dysfunctional, and yes, it left scarring internal and external.

Like it or not, fair or not, for me to make sure I only had people in my life who were kind, loving, safe, and equal. I had personal work to do, and lots of it, so I did it and felt even freer.

As someone who is on the other side …. I can tell you no matter how dark it seems, no matter what experiences you have that have scorned your heart or your trust, you will recover.

Be peaceful with yourself; time will be on your side, love is available, and your soul will become wise and understand things you may not understand now.

There are good people in the world, and they will one day be in your inner circle.

I practiced internal resilience, and sometimes, I don't know where it came from. I wasn't versed at that time in my life on meditation or any of the practices I use today. I think it was a deep sense that I had more to live for and wanted the "dream life" one day .. the family, the love, and a beautiful life.

I saw other people who didn't have violence in their life, so that meant I could too.

Holding onto and not letting my dreams die of a different future life gave me resilience.

Just keep working on you.
Keep loving you.
Don't let it take your kindness.
Don't let it take you hope.

And my dear sister or brother survivor….,
Love, love, love, love yourself.

My greatest therapy has been music …. find yours.

Be well and stay groovy.

｜ Deb Drummond

Devin Gambler

Born of poverty, homelessness, and multiple failures in academia, I still achieved my dream, my MBA.

Navigating the journey to achieve my MBA was as if the odds were stacked against me. You see, I wasn't an academic and came from humble beginnings. Coming from a background marked by poverty & struggle, my early years were spent navigating the challenges of being homeless and moving through the foster care system as a youth. These experiences gave me a resilience that was both a necessity for survival and a foundation for future endeavors. Despite this, I held true to a dream of being someone who would one day lead & make a difference.

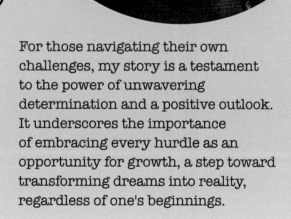

For those navigating their own challenges, my story is a testament to the power of unwavering determination and a positive outlook. It underscores the importance of embracing every hurdle as an opportunity for growth, a step toward transforming dreams into reality, regardless of one's beginnings.

The role of a single parent to two boys, at times relying on the support of my mother, added layers of complexity and responsibility to my life. A single mom raised me, so I see how hard that could be. Therefore, the endeavor to pursue higher education was not just a personal goal but a beacon of hope and a testament to the possibility of transcending one's circumstances.

Balancing fatherhood with the demands of an MBA program was a profound challenge, particularly when my youngest son was born in the early weeks of my studies. The nights spent caring for him, followed by exhaustive study sessions, epitomized the relentless drive and perseverance that had become second nature to me. "Embrace the grind" became more than a mantra; it was a lived experience reflecting my journey from the streets to the academic halls.

My family's support and understanding were crucial, especially my wife's unwavering dedication. This journey was a collective endeavor, with every sacrifice and achievement woven into the fabric of our family's blanket. Pursuing my MBA was imbued with the weight of my past and the aspirations for my family's future, driving me forward against all odds.

They're watching everyone who is counting on you, from your kids to nephews, nieces, family, people who want to see you fail & tell you "Good luck." I knew I couldn't fail & so I dedicated more time and attention to courses that were tough and leaned on my classmates in areas that were weaknesses of mine. The one course, Business Finance, was one of the reasons why I never achieved a business degree. I worked so hard and eked out a B-. You are only allowed one; it was my make or break & it didn't break me.

My cohort started with 20 students. I saw some really good people, and that life happened for them, and they dropped out. We became a close group & helped each other out. One student saved me on one of my weaker courses. I phoned her up & was at my wit's end and so frustrated on a final assignment. She was patient, explained everything on how to do the assignment, and followed up with the outline she used in an email. I would have failed that course. She passed away two months before the program ended. I realize now that she was in a lot of pain with Chemotherapy and still answered the call. I owe her what she did and am inspired by her selflessness. I am currently working for her nation.

Reflecting on this arduous path, resilience shines through not just in enduring but thriving amidst adversity. For those navigating their own challenges, my story is a testament to the power of unwavering determination and a positive outlook. It underscores the importance of embracing every hurdle as an opportunity for growth, a step toward transforming dreams into reality, regardless of one's beginnings.

My people's watchful eyes fueled my resilience; failing wasn't an option - this was always bigger than me. I would like to leave you with this piece of advice: never lose sight of your vision and the gifts you have been given.

Devin Gambler

Godsway Tek Agyagbo

Resilience reared its head for me when I had to resign from a job I had known and loved all my life because the organization's failure victimized me.

I had felt my life had come to an end, with hopelessness, devastation, feelings of guilt, and self-blame. For a long period of 15 months, I was consumed with feelings of anger, resentment, and a loss of trust in others or myself.

I had to move far away from home, family, and friends to process all that had happened, even though I had seen it coming years before. Relocating and seeking peace and sanity with my best friend, Osbert, was my first step, and that has kept me alive today. I was broke, had no job, and no energy and purpose to find a new job, all amidst my already challenging emotional state.

Never forget that even if all family members and trusted friends forsake you or victimize you, find a way to open up yourself to be loved whenever the chance presents itself. If you can, go out and treat yourself, drink with a friend or random person. Keep your mind open to only those who pour positive vibes into your dark moments.

Isolation, loneliness, loss of purpose, and identity took me into the darkest moments of my life: depression. I became suicidal; I had attempted to take my life twice but got saved. My best friend Osbert's apartment was on the 4th floor, so imagine the fear and sleepless nights I put my friend through.

I took a job, alas, as a delivery boy, and my love for motorbikes made it an easier decision, even though I know some of my friends made fun of me (from grace to grass). I remember some days on the highways while riding to deliver parcels to clients, and I would purposely ride in front of heavy trucks in pursuit of ending my life. Again, I got saved by the owner of the car, who knocked me off my bike with only a scratch on my hands and knees.

One day, I parked the delivery motorbike under a footbridge, walked up the bridge, and stood there, gathering the courage to jump. A homeless boy who had thought he could get some coins from me kept pulling my shirt and signaling me to give him money for food. I gave this boy (about seven years old) all my sales money from my delivery sales that day.

It was then I realized I could do some good again. It was on that same bridge my friend and mentor, Elizabeth Wolf, messaged me and said she was willing to support me with a monthly allowance to keep me going because I hated the delivery job even though I loved that I had a motorbike at my disposal.

The only job that gives me meaning is working with kids and young people, and that got taken away from me.

I don't know how I coped exactly, but I survived because my friend Osbert took me in for 13 months. I didn't have to contribute to bills or buy food, and I had free internet. So, the moment Elizabeth Wolf started sending me my monthly allowance, I had hope. Then she visited Ghana and took me on a vacation while playing tour guide, my second favorite job, which has become a side business since Elizabeth's visit. While kayaking on the Volta Lake with Elizabeth and her daughter Samantha, the idea of an after-school center settled on me.

Another friend I am grateful for is Ali Francis; he isn't just an incredible friend; he's like a brother. He's always been there for me through thick and thin, offering a listening ear without judgment. I remember vividly how, when I confided in him about [specific struggle], he surprised me by starting a monthly allowance that continues to this day.

His generosity extends far beyond finances. He donated computers to my after-school center, treated hardworking kids to celebratory dinners, and even surprised me with unforgettable vacations. Every gesture, big or small, speaks volumes about his caring nature and unwavering support. I'm incredibly grateful to have him in my life.

I am alive today because my friends supported and loved me until my dreams of working with young people came to light. That was hope. That was life again.

I started reading books again when confronted with this challenge and the need to practice resilience. I got back online, researching ways to bring global volunteers and travelers down to my village in Ghana to support some of my youth development projects.

I started writing partnership proposal letters and emails, contacting universities, high schools, and organizations in Europe and North America.

Working daily towards launching an after-school center in my village made me tough. It made me withstand the darkness of depression.

Never forget that even if all family members and trusted friends forsake you or victimize you, find a way to open up yourself to be loved whenever the chance presents itself. If you can, go out and treat yourself, drink with a friend or random person. Keep your mind open to only those who pour positive vibes into your dark moments.

Godsway Tek Agyagbo

Hamza Najam

Alcohol and drug addiction had taken over my life. I could not go a day without drinking a bottle of wine or six cans of beer. I had been trying to stop for five years but failed every time and was in a very bad place in life. I had lost my friends, I was broke, and I was almost about to lose my job.

At the age of 19, I moved to Canada. On paper, it was to get a better education than I would back home. The real mission, though, was to complete my education, make something out of myself, and pave the way for my parents and brother to move to Canada in search of a more comfortable life.

I had to find my own way, work minimum wage jobs, pay $20,000/year in tuition fees, and put a roof over my head without any work experience or any family in Canada, all at the age of 19.

Once I got here, things shifted quickly, and the allure of the underground party scene in Toronto consumed me quickly. I thought I was just having fun...I always had the work hard, play hard mentality.

Before I knew it, alcohol and drugs became a big part of my identity, a constant presence in my daily life. I would drink to celebrate, drink when I was upset, drink because it's the evening, binge drink with my friends, binge drink at home for no reason... I found any excuse to have a drink.

By the time I was 30, the mission was far from complete, and I had not met my parents in nearly a decade.

Practicing resilience for me looked like learning to sit with my painful emotions each time I craved a drink. I learned to practice self-love by enduring the cravings because I knew it was for my highest good. I cut out all distractions of going out, socializing, and feeling like I was missing out because I knew I had to do this.

I was drinking every day, indulging in drugs every weekend, and spiraling into a pit of depression, financial instability, and self-loathing. I hated who I had become and hated being in my own skin. I felt alone; not having met my family for so long took its toll on me. I was the black sheep of my family, and I had become the laughingstock.

I had this overwhelming sense of failure like I let my family down and my brother down, and because of me, they may never have a shot at a better life.

No matter how hard I tried, I felt alone and could not find love or happiness. This kept me firmly in the throes of alcohol addiction.

I was caught in a vicious cycle, a carousel of self-destruction that I couldn't seem to escape. I tried to quit multiple times, but each attempt ended in failure. I was trapped; the more I struggled, the deeper I sank. Nothing seemed to work. After going to AA meetings, outpatient programs, and therapy, I had nearly given up.

But on March 11, 2020, I decided to make one last attempt. I picked up a book, "Breaking The Habit of Being Yourself," which was like a beacon of light in the darkness. I realized that I was the architect of my own misery, and only I had the power to dismantle it. Dr Joe Dispenza introduced me to the quantum world of energies and the idea of manifesting the exact reality you want. This realization was a turning point for me. It lit a fire in my belly.

The first month of sobriety was a battle. I grappled with withdrawals, my hands shook uncontrollably, and anxiety was my constant companion. Sleep was elusive; I was exhausted but held on, drawing upon an inner strength I didn't know I possessed.

I took it one day at a time, and slowly, I saw a glimmer of light at the end of the tunnel. I started to love myself again.

As the world struggled with the COVID-19 pandemic, I saw the devastating impact it was having on people's mental health.

I saw good people succumbing to the pressures of isolation, turning to alcohol as a crutch. I saw an increase in stress and anxiety on a global scale and a sharp decline in mental health. This is when I realized I could do more than just help myself; I could help others just like me.

Three months into my sobriety, I found my calling. I became fascinated with neuroscience and its power in effecting change in the brain. I reinvented myself as a Sobriety Coach and Meditation Teacher, earning certifications in Neuroscience, Meditation, Neuro-Linguistic Programming, Breathwork, and Alcohol Recovery Coaching. I was determined to use my experience and newfound knowledge to help others.

The Hard Reset Method was born. (Later became Breathesober™.

By January 2021, I created a novel program designed to help people create an alcohol-free lifestyle. I started changing hundreds of lives, using mindfulness and sobriety as my tools. I was no longer a victim of my addiction; I was a beacon of hope for others struggling with their own.

Today, we have a thriving community of over 1500 members, actively working towards sobriety or living an amazing, alcohol-free life.

In the process of helping others, I transformed my own life. I quadrupled my income, found the love of my life, lost weight, and became a pillar of strength for hundreds of others. I was no longer the man who was defined by his addiction; I was the man who had overcome it and was using his experience to help others do the same. The big difference? I absolutely loved who I had become. I loved the person I saw in the mirror.

Looking back, I realize that my journey was not just about overcoming addiction. It was about rediscovering my strength, reclaiming my life, and redefining my identity. It was about breaking the habit of being myself and becoming who I was meant to be.

Today, I stand tall, not as a victim, but as a survivor. Today, I am 1244 days Sober. I spend my days healing others, helping them release their trauma and find peace with an alcohol-free life. My brother is in Canada, and my parents can come and go as they wish. I am living the life I once could only dream of.

I am a testament to the power of change, the strength of the human spirit, and the resilience of the mind. I am a source of healing and change for those still trapped in the throes of addiction, living proof that it's never too late to change your life.

My journey has taught me that we all have a light inside of us, that we have the power to change, and that it's never too late to start over. It has taught me that we are not defined by our past but by our choices, actions, and determination to create a better future.

And for that, I am forever grateful.

Practicing resilience for me looked like learning to sit with my painful emotions each time I craved a drink. I learned to practice self-love by enduring the cravings because I knew it was for my highest good. I cut out all distractions of going out, socializing, and feeling like I was missing out because I knew I had to do this.

Alcohol is not the problem; it is a symptom of a deeper problem. Without uncovering and addressing this deeper-rooted problem, true freedom will be hard to come by.

Hamza Najam

Heather Marianna

I suffered a deep depression after my relationship ended, and my name was being exploited in my very successful business.

I grew up with a heart that believed in the inherent goodness of people. I was often too trusting and too kind for my own good. But as life unfolded, 2023 would be the year when I finally realized that not everyone shared my pure intentions. It was a harsh awakening that I needed to shake off the issues I had been concealing for years.

The year 2023, without a doubt, stands as one of the most challenging chapters in my life story. My life's love departed, leaving an irreplaceable void in my heart. I had thought he was "the one," and the revelation of his true nature shattered my world. The entire relationship had been a facade, a lie I struggled to accept. I became entangled in a personal hell where fixing the relationship consumed me entirely. Everything else fell by the wayside, including self-care, my fitness routine, and my passion for work and beloved companies. I felt like I was drowning in despair.

I took a drastic step and sought help from a therapist and healer. Through their guidance, I began to see that I had done nothing wrong. I was merely entangled with a narcissist, and that realization was the first glimmer of hope after months of darkness. As the first part of the year drew to a close, I started feeling better, only for another bombshell to hit me.

I had taken a company public, but it soon became evident that my partners were exploiting my name and brand for their own gain. I had poured nearly three years of my life and a significant investment of half a million dollars into a project that crumbled beneath my feet, largely due to the shady actions of the CEO. Depression cast a relentless shadow over me, and thoughts of despair visited me regularly.

I practiced resilience through meditation, prayer, and a lot of outdoor activity. I also shut the TV off a lot and tried to get more one with myself and begin to learn to be alone. I also practice huge amounts of discernment when working with anyone new, and I shut people out at the first sign of something being off.

My message to anyone facing their own trials is a simple yet powerful one. It all begins with mindset. Take a step back from everyone and work on yourself first. Everything everything else can wait.

Depression may try to consume us, but I refuse to be a victim of my circumstances. I am the Comeback Queen, and my resilience will carry me through any storm.

I've endured trials and hardships that few know about. I've survived an abusive relationship, battled the manipulation of a narcissist, and faced adversity that could have broken me. But here I stand, a living testament to the unwavering strength of resilience.

I practiced resilience through meditation, prayer, and a lot of outdoor activity. I also shut the TV off a lot and tried to get more one with myself and begin to learn to be alone. I also practice huge amounts of discernment when working with anyone new, and I shut people out at the first sign of something being off.

Heather Marianna

Amidst this darkness, a realization emerged. These people, including my ex, couldn't take anything from me. I had crafted my life and my story, and not to mention most of their success was built on my network. The last quarter of the year brought a remarkable turn of events. I found myself booked for a role in a holiday movie set for 2024 – a dream come true. I was also working on several celebrity events, planning a trip to Africa and co-producing an event for the Oscars. These were just the tip of the iceberg; much more was on the horizon. I aligned with incredible women, and 2024 was beginning to look amazing.

As I prepared to welcome the new year, my heart brimmed with love and gratitude, leaving behind the hurt that had consumed me. I had turned the corner.

I embarked on a journey of self-discovery, shedding the burdens that had weighed me down for so long. I rediscovered my strength and belief in myself. At 45, I faced the daunting task of rebuilding my emotions and starting anew. Yet, I knew each day was a gift, an opportunity to create something extraordinary. I was blessed with a supportive circle of friends and invaluable resources to navigate the toughest days.

Jaleh Zandieh

After graduate school, I moved to China and wanted to do a good job in my work in a new city, a new country, another culture, and a new language. I became completely overwhelmed with doubt while planning my first bilingual fundraising event that was very close to my heart, and I didn't want to let anyone down.

I was a 24-year-old graduate from the University of the Sciences in Philadelphia and moved to Zhenjiang, China, to work for an international non-profit organization. My role as a cultural ambassador allowed me to use my new master's degree to work with local children who didn't have their own families.

It took time to get used to so many new things, and I felt months passing so quickly. My Mandarin language skills weren't great, but daily conversations were becoming easier. Instead of a tourist, I felt like I was now part of the city. My friends and neighbors helped build my confidence. One day, I woke up and believed I was in the right place, part of a community, doing meaningful work I loved. I felt at home.

I wanted to keep building on the momentum of so much immersive learning in my new city and focus on doing more service projects for a place I resonated with. So, I decided to extend my contract.

I asked myself questions to gain clarity:
"How can I use my time well?"
"What would make a positive impact on the children here?"
"What would my future self want me to do?"

Time felt like a precious resource passing quickly, and I wanted to use it well. Adoption had always been something I cared about. My first childhood friends were adopted from other countries. We were neighbors, and our families were close. Their parents raised them in loving homes and with opportunities to develop their potential. Having different physical features than their parents wasn't a barrier to being completely embraced and accepted. They were loved and fully seen.

What if I could help more kids have loving, adopted families like that?

This was the clear nudge I asked for. While working at a local center that provided services to children who didn't have families of their own, I asked:

"What do they need?
"What would create new opportunities for them to have happy, healthy lives?

Over a conversation at a teahouse, new ideas flowed:

"What if we made a fundraiser for the children and had local artists perform?
"Could we showcase the diverse talents and cultures of people from Zhenjiang and foreigners living there?

The event was called *"East Meets West,"* we wanted it to unite people of all backgrounds to enjoy an evening of the arts and donate all of the money to children in need.

The team was made up of friends who volunteered to share their time, resources, art, talents, and expertise. We also got sponsors who made donations for the event.

During initial conversations, I had a rush of energy and ideas. My goal went BIG – a program of performances that went above and beyond people's expectations that led to standing ovations. I visualized the elation of reaching our financial goal and giving the money to the medical director of the children's center. Our biggest motivation was imagining the faces of our Cutie Pies, who could now be one step closer to being adopted.

Trust that solutions present themselves in all types of ways: through new ideas, through loved ones, trustworthy experts, kindhearted friends, nourishing communities, wise teachers, gifts, strangers, and joyful invitations.

We wanted to have a room filled with people who care about improving the quality of life of children **and** who value the arts. Any event with these ingredients would *have* to be a success, right? When this was my focus, I felt that anything was possible. The vision was right there for us to create and make a reality.

Then suddenly, thoughts deviated into doubt, and heaviness set in. There was **so** much to do! People were asking me so many questions, and they each needed answers. The excitement ripple dwindled and was replaced and outmatched by waves of uncertainty that lingered. A doubtful train of thoughts played on a repeat loop, like an annoying song that won't stop.

"What if this doesn't work out?
"What if I let everyone down?
"What if no one buys a ticket?
"What if people show up but hate the program?
"Do people want a fundraiser?
"What makes me think I can do this?
"I've never done something like this before.
"I'm only 24! How can I be in charge?
"Did I reach too high?
"Why should people help me when I'm so green?
"What if I don't know the answers to people's questions?
"I don't know how to create a bilingual event!

I remembered my goal:
To co-create something beautiful and dignified for the people of Zhenjiang.

I remembered why it's important:
I fell in love with the kids there and wanted to give them a gift since working with them changed my life. We were doing this event with service and love – love for the diverse cultures being celebrated, the city we all lived in, and the children who would receive more tomorrow than they had yesterday.

I decided to welcome creative solutions that would make this adventure even better than we initially planned. I looked for clues that solutions were coming our way.

I remembered I wasn't alone.

My friends reminded me that we're a team and we'll be successful together.

Knowing how to ask for help was never easy for me, but I realized I had an all-star team. I said goodbye to the notion that I needed to figure everything out myself.

The team had various strengths and leadership styles that blended and harmonized well. We each contributed uniquely to creating a fundraiser designed to improve our little brothers' and sisters' quality of life. We may not be related to them, but we related to their needs since we all share the same ones.

A special quote from Bahá'u'lláh that was always a source of hope for me added inspiration:

"So powerful is the light of unity that it can illuminate the whole earth."

Our team's unity added more light to our special city and part of the world. We could be like instruments playing in tune with each other... for everyone's higher good. That's the beauty of service and community... a powerful type of unity that didn't erase any of our unique distinctions. Everyone could be fully seen, valued, and contribute.

I sought out bridge-builders and trustworthy leaders who care about others and were fueled by service. Each added a solution and opened another door or connection. We created a community rooted in trust.

There were four pillars of my resilience: A meaningful goal that lit up my heart with joy, having a team who trusted each other, harmonizing everyone's strengths, and actively finding solutions to accomplish new and difficult things.

Two artists gave me Chinese calligraphy paintings that visually represented pillars of resilience:

Trust | Perseverance | Peace

Resilience needs trust, perseverance, and peace.

- Trust yourself in difficult times.
- Perseverance is a practice of courageous dedication to pursue your goal.
- Peace is the capacity to be steady during shaky situations.

I remembered that I wasn't alone. People showed up to help me. They wanted us to succeed. We created a unified vision so everyone could co-create a joyful, vibrant, and inclusive experience to inspire everyone.

Focusing on the meaningful goal and combining the talents of dedicated people allowed us to create magic together. Progress was the key -- not perfection.

相信 (Trust)

毅力 (Perseverance)

和平 (Peace)

Tell yourself - as often as needed - that there are keys that open every lock. Every challenge has solutions. A speed bump is *part* of the road but not the *actual* road. Stay focused on the road and how you can set yourself up to see the next solution.

Trust that solutions present themselves in all types of ways: through new ideas, through loved ones, trustworthy experts, kindhearted friends, nourishing communities, wise teachers, gifts, strangers, and joyful invitations.

You're never alone, and there are good people everywhere.

Jaleh Zandieh

Jazzamyn Walker

At 28, my father's unexpected passing became the pivotal moment that propelled me into being the resilient woman I am today.

My head rested on my dad's chest as he drew his final breath. He passed away surrounded by family, except for his mother, who chose to pray with a congregation. The loss of a second child within a year and a half was unbearable for her. My dad had suffered an anoxic Brain Injury while alone in his apartment and was found by military police several days later, barely alive. As his next of kin, I was burdened with the decision to withdraw life support.

Grief can't be quantified. Take your time and be gentle with yourself. You'll know when you're ready to step back into your power.

When I mustered the strength to open my eyes, I saw the nurse outside our ICU room signaling that my dad had passed away.

It was then that I realized the linchpin holding our family together was gone. My biggest supporter, the person who challenged me the most and the one I leaned on for major decisions, was no longer with us. It was time for me to step up. Leaving my family with him, I immediately initiated calls about organ donation, contacted the coroner, and reached out to the Military Cemetery to discuss my dad's funeral plans.

Upon returning home after a few weeks away, the adjustment was difficult. I've unfortunately experienced loss many times in my life. I had a dedicated funeral outfit by the age of 13 that saw plenty of use. Death wasn't unfamiliar to me, but this loss was unique. This marked the second time I grieved the loss of my father. The initial time was when he returned home from his last military deployment, and I realized the version of my father who had raised me was lost overseas. The new version I got to know coincided with my journey into womanhood. Consequently, our strong bond deepened as we became equals and friends. Losing him was not just losing a father but also losing my best friend.

This event shattered me and fundamentally changed who I am. The person I was before his passing ceased to exist with him. I could no longer rely on him to bail me out of tough situations, financially support me, or validate my decisions. I was on my own, and I could no longer exist as a 28-year-old girl with a safety net of a father.

I felt myself crumbling inward. Fragile, anxious, wounded, grappling with abandonment issues, family drama, and the realization of my job instability. I attempted activities that previously brought me joy, but living in a grey storm cloud made it challenging to see the world in color.

A girl I'd recently met at a summer music festival encouraged me about the accessories I'd been creating, suggesting I start a business. As a successful business owner herself, she mentored me, igniting the realization that I had to take charge of my life and that entrepreneurship could offer financial freedom.

Nearly a year passed before the autopsy results revealed the cause of my dad's death. Years of alcohol abuse had impacted his heart, leading to his demise. Determined not to follow that path, I resolved to confront my trauma, abandon self-medication through drugs and alcohol, and acquire coping skills.

My journey of self-discovery and improvement began in mid-2020. Regular visits to a psychiatrist, therapist, and family doctor led to multiple diagnoses, shedding light on my brain's workings and my emotional responses. Engaging in various therapy modalities like DBT, CBT, EMDR, and more, I shared this journey on my business's social platforms. I firmly believe that increased awareness about ADHD, Autism, BPD, Clinical Depression, General Anxiety, and more could have prevented my undiagnosed status for 28 years. Understanding my brain has allowed me to view myself with greater compassion, realizing my "flaws" were unmanaged symptoms of invisible disabilities.

This realization has shaped my business today. It's not just about creating beautiful, sparkling accessories to mask my depression but about providing accessibility for those with invisible disabilities. We're establishing a safe space for marginalized communities, fostering an understanding of different brains to encourage self-compassion and empathy toward others.

While my dad's death was the most devastating event in my life, his absence sculpted me into the woman I am today. I've grown beyond what I could have ever imagined in my wildest dreams.

I truly believe that being resilient is an act of self-love. By genuinely allowing myself to experience my emotions, I was able to redirect that grief into a sense of purpose.

Grief can't be quantified. Take your time and be gentle with yourself. You'll know when you're ready to step back into your power.

Jazzamyn Walker

Jess Kelly

Over the course of my life, I have had to demonstrate resilience a lot. The time that comes to mind first was when I got the phone call that my mother had died after undergoing elective surgery in Victoria, Brazil.

It's 2005. I'm 21 years old. I'd recently moved out of the house and married my high school sweetheart. I work as an assistant manager at a clothing store in the mall. I am finishing my associate's degree at the community college and preparing to transfer to the university. I'm in the thick of young adulthood. My mom and I are exploring a new type of relationship now that I am out of the house.

I'd spent much of my life listening to my mother's issues and problems about her weight. She'd had gastric bypass surgery a few years before. She'd lost a considerable amount of weight and, as a result, had a lot of loose skin. We spent what seemed like months talking about places she wanted to go to fix this. She wanted to feel as good about what she saw on the outside as she did about the inside. I thought the idea of going overseas was just a fantasy. I didn't think it would ever really be a reality. I was wrong.

If you have something you've shoved down deep in your life, it's never too late to peel the layers back and process it.

It's Thanksgiving. We all went to her place. Nothing from the day stands out to me. I can't recall the food or the conversation. I do remember the goodbye. She seems anxious and very excited. She is going to Brazil with another woman from her weight loss support group. This was it, her key to solving the biggest issue of her life. She'd received a recent inheritance from her mother's death. There was no stopping her. She was finally going to feel good. We hugged. My mom was a fantastic hugger. She held me just a touch longer than normal, and we said goodbye. That was our final physical moment together.

After that, I went home. I worked a hectic weekend at the mall and busied myself studying for exams the following week. I woke up from a strange dream about my mom and realized I hadn't heard from my stepfather about mom's surgery yet. After class, I called him. He was frantic and searching for his passport. He said that the doctor called and that they thought he needed to come. They were unsure what was happening, but it didn't look good. I told him I could go. I had a passport. He got another call. As I sat in the garage awaiting his call back, I had this horrible feeling that my mom was going to die alone. Moments later, the phone rang. She was gone.

Initially, my feelings and reaction to this were pure and utter devastation.

After losing my father just three years before, I felt overwhelmed. Orphaned at 21. Panic mode and fog quickly turned into "doer" mode. I had to put all of my feelings aside because someone had to deal with all of the paperwork and logistics of an overseas death. I felt numb because of the sheer sense of responsibility for doing these big things—numbness to protect the little girl inside who had just lost her mother.

When it came to coping, there were a lot of strategies, but mostly, I was in denial. I didn't deal with it. I put it in a box tucked deeply into my subconscious. I took quick peeks inside over the years, but most of those were when I was in an altered state of consciousness. Getting drunk or smoking weed was a continual negative outlet. Otherwise, sober me was afraid, unwilling, and unequipped to face the challenge of dealing with this.

A lot of things went through my mind over the years. Now, almost 18 years later, I still have so many questions. Was she in pain? What did the timeline of events that led to her death actually look like? Was she scared? Did she know she was dying? What was she thinking in the end? These thoughts were always in continual loops that felt like they would never close.

I started talking about them with my therapist. We started really diving into the loss and my feelings about it. I began thinking about the woman that was with Mom. Could I find her? Could I get some of these answers? With a bit of research and another bit of luck, I found her through her granddaughter on Facebook. We exchanged phone numbers and email addresses. I wrote a long email including a list of questions and hit send…. I waited.

After a few weeks with no reply, I began to get anxious. Maybe she didn't want to talk to me about this. Maybe it was too much? I decided the best way to approach this was as directly as possible. I sent her a message asking about the email. She explained that she'd tried to sit down and respond to the email, but the answers were complicated. We scheduled a call.

When the time came to talk, I had a lot of mixed feelings. I was anxious. Would I get the answers I was looking for? The call felt awkward at first, but we soon found it easy to talk to one another. She spoke with me about the last days of my mother's life. She shared fun stories of their last conversations eating seafood at a beach cafe. My mom was excited and very determined. We talked about all the questions and more. She helped me close a lot of the loops. Hearing the answers to some of those questions was hard, really hard in some ways. But having them closed and having a sense of knowing has really helped me move forward in my grief.

To practice resilience, I did what I needed to do to navigate my life without my mom. Unfortunately, that meant not facing these challenges until just recently. I have now been practicing a thing my therapist called, and I describe as a type of delayed resilience. An understanding that during the time of her death, I was not able to really process it, but now I am ready.

Sometimes, things are too difficult to deal with in the moment that they happen in our lives. Sometimes, our minds subconsciously package them away because they know we aren't ready to handle them. Even though it took me 18 years to really dive deep and process my mother's death, I am still resilient. I am still growing and changing through the experience. I can also tell that younger version of myself that it's ok. She did what she could at the time. If you have something you've shoved down deep in your life, it's never too late to peel the layers back and process it.

Jess Kelly

Jessica Emich

I was diagnosed with a serious autoimmune disease. They said I may end up in a wheelchair and advised me not to have another child.

After a long and somber conversation with the doctor, I was handed a bottle of pills and a pamphlet. Before my hand even reached the door handle to leave, I had already decided this would not be my story.

When I was a teenager, I would often have pain in my hips. I just dealt with it and chalked it up as residual misalignment from being a gymnast for many years. As I got older, through my college years, it bothered me so much at times that I would occasionally walk with a limp. I did not like that as I was healthy and active!

Fast forward to my adult years. I was married and the mother to one little girl. I wanted another, as I am a triplet, one of three sisters, and I have an older brother. Family and siblings mean everything to me. We tried for over a year to get pregnant. Throughout this time, the pain in my hips was happening more often and felt more severe. I finally decided to see a doctor, which led to many tests and concerned looks. Eventually, they diagnosed me with a serious autoimmune disease. "It will only get worse," they said. "Pregnancy is not a good idea," they warned. And on and on. But a loud voice from deep within me said-No freaking way am I settling for that reality.

So there I was, having gotten my Masters in Nutrition, a trained energy worker, a yoga teacher, athletic, a wife, a mother, and a diagnosis. I felt shame that I had what I thought was the knowledge to heal from something like this. These things helped, but nothing really worked to heal me completely. I felt defeated but also determined. I started to think about the energetics of an autoimmune disease- the body attacking itself. I got very real with myself. I began tuning into my body. I began tuning into the places that hurt. I leaned into the pain. I saw myself when it all began. The messages were coming in loud and clear. This stemmed from my lack of self-love, my abandonment of self-acceptance, my overriding feeling of needing to be "perfect" to be worthy.

Why did I have these feelings? I grew up in a loving family. I had a husband that adored me. I had a healthy baby that brought me so much joy. As I allowed myself to dive into the depths I normally avoid (without even realizing it), I realized that I wasn't really letting my life nourish me. My heart was armored. I was not allowing myself to feel. I was in full protection mode.

I began to drop into the wisdom of my body. It moved me from my overthinking mind into my feeling heart. I began to learn a new language- the language of the body. I listened, lovingly, patiently. Things began to bubble to the surface. I practiced softening in the wake of it rather than denying the experience and lodging it in my body. I began to understand that I am so much more than my physicality, stories, and programs. I started to unshackle myself from the past and become present, like really present. I began to see how life was gifting me everything in my path to open me to my true essence, my divinity. The divinity that we all are that everything is. I started to get a bird's eye view, which helped me see the wonder and beauty of my experience. I fell more and more in love with myself. I fell more in love with everything around me. It was a rebirth of sorts. A new perspective

Presently, I am in a whole new body. I no longer have symptoms of that disease. As I raise my two daughters, I continue to practice feeling my heart and opening to presence. I began to let my life evolve me rather than trying to overly control it.

Step by step, I started to open, to let the armor down, to feel. It had to begin with how I truly felt about myself. I practiced rising to meet what arose in my life with presence and patience. I let it be the medicine in my life for healing and opening deeper parts of myself.

Physical and emotional pain can be a portal to awakening us to our wholeness if we let it. Healing is a journey – a beautiful journey because it is the journey toward knowing ourselves more deeply. And the more we know ourselves, the more we inevitably love ourselves and understand and embody our divinity.

As we lean into our challenges, letting them evolve us by listening deeply and slowing down to be present with our pain. Recognizing this is our being calling us toward awakening to more parts of ourselves.

This is how we become our own healers and connect to our true essence. And that is living a life filled with love and freedom. It begins within.

Jessica Emich

> As we lean into our challenges, letting them evolve us by listening deeply and slowing down to be present with our pain. Recognizing this is our being calling us toward awakening to more parts of ourselves.

Step by step, I started to open, to let the armor down, to feel. It had to begin with how I truly felt about myself. For some reason, I always had this feeling that I was not enough or not worthy of having a gigantically amazing life. I know that this stemmed from my not loving and accepting myself. Once we learn to love and accept ourselves, we can receive that love from elsewhere. From everywhere- nature, family, community, pets, strangers. Everywhere!. But it begins within, and it begins with the self.

So, how did I learn to love myself? Several ways. I would picture myself during my early teen years and love her back to life, to fullness. I reframed all the things that I started judging myself about. I began seeing her as courageous, sensitive, and beautiful.

Jessica Munoz

I had a dream to create a place of healing for a marginalized and vulnerable population of children who are often invisible to society. This dream became a reality after a 15-year journey, arduous seed planting, and multiple obstacles.

You practice resilience every day-the moment you decide to get out of bed, put your feet on the floor, keep persevering, find your fortitude and the depth of your grit, and remain committed to carrying the torch forward. Sometimes, you also need to take a break.

Fifteen years ago, my world was flipped upside down when, through my day job as a trauma nurse, children who were being mislabeled and abused, sexually exploited, and underrecognized as victims of child sex trafficking came into my world. I thought my role was solely to raise awareness of this hidden issue amongst my healthcare colleagues, but then the reality of the plight of these children became clear. The depth of the systemic issues that lead to victimization, the lack of empathy, and a comprehensive continuum of care became apparent. I developed this relentless ache in my core for these children, and the activated justice gene on my DNA mandated my action... I envisioned a place of healing where girls who had been victimized could heal. Such a place didn't exist. Healing of body, mind, spirit, and emotion... Transformative life-changing healing. My calling to shine the light into the darkness and watch new life come forth became my mantra. I had no idea "how" to build this place, but I knew the end goal of what was needed.

I am not originally from Hawaii, but this was where I had been planted and the roots of where my work helping these children were seeded. Hawaii is beautiful, the land of aloha, beautiful sunsets, and beaches. Still, it also has a very dark side with vulnerable populations such as children who are being sex trafficked. Being a blonde-haired, blue-eyed outsider carries with it, very unique challenges, not only in developing an organization and business but also in raising funds, capacity, community buy-in, connections, and gaining overall acceptance. Then, layer on an issue that carries with it taboo and shame and is one of our time's hardest and most challenging topics. Oh, and maintain your full-time job in the emergency room to pay your bills. I really had no idea what I was stepping into: the sabotage attempts, the promises that didn't come to fruition, and challenging relationships. Likely, if I had known, I wouldn't have taken the leap of faith to do SOMETHING. If I had not taken that leap, I would never have experienced the most incredible front-row seat and first-hand experience with divine miracles and connections. I also would have never learned the vital lessons about being patient. "No doesn't always mean no. It often means not yet". Timing is everything. My faith would not be what it is today!

The good, the bad, the challenges, the failures, and the triumphs have all played a part in galvanizing the resilience in my soul. I told myself many times, "This is too much," "I can't do this anymore," "The road is too bumpy, and the mountains keep getting taller to climb," "Can everyone stop putting more rocks in my backpack to carry. This is too heavy already!". When these thoughts would come racing in as my head hit the pillow each night, I would think of the hundreds of children out there, being exploited, living on the streets, and remind myself WHY I had to keep going and that no matter what I went through it would never carry the weight of what one day, one hour, one minute in the day of the life of one of these kids. The least I could do was use my voice to disrupt in the name of safety and healing, keep pioneering, keep carrying the torch, shining the light until people could no longer look away, and inspire them to action, believing that together, we can bring transformational change for children.

Millions of tears and prayers have sprinkled the ground of what is now known as Pearl Haven: A Place of Healing. Even to this day, when I pull in the gate and breathe in the serenity and anointing of this space, I am humbled and honored to have been tasked with doing what many thought would be impossible. This work has gone through many seasons, just as my personal journey has walked parallel to those seasons. When you are a Founder, the parallel becomes intertwined. I believe, while it's not always the best scenario, it is what gives you the resolve to keep going. The girls I am blessed to walk alongside as they embrace the hard road of facing their trauma and choosing to heal, remind me daily of the power and the magnitude of true resilient hope.

You practice resilience every day- the moment you decide to get out of bed, put your feet on the floor, keep persevering, find your fortitude and the depth of your grit, and remain committed to carrying the torch forward. Sometimes, you also need to take a break.

Seasons are just that... seasons. Temporary. Transitional. Transformative. The seasons feel like refining fire, galvanizing deep-seated resilience, grit, and grace.

Jesssica Munoz

Jill Emich

Problem? Who am I,
and what do I REALLY want?

Solution - The answer lies within.

> I do something to raise my joy meter instead of staying stuck in a funk. I keep coming back to the words, "Change my energy, change my life." It has been HUGELY helpful. Life is an INside job, after all.

I am the middle sister of triplets, two eggs, one split, and I am the creation of one of those split eggs. My story is about finding my own unique voice & purpose FINALLY. A quest, I believe, that is vital for each and every one of us.

Being one of three has had incredible blessings. For instance, growing up, we always had someone to play with. We never had to go to our first day of kindergarten or our first day of college alone. We were so attuned to each other that it felt totally natural to be together. It was all we knew.

Being in the middle, I learned how to keep the peace. I was a hardcore people-pleaser, and it played out in all my relationships. The upside was that I had a lot of friends and was always game to bring the good vibes and the good times. It played out in dating where I would be everything I thought they wanted me to be, my people-pleaser avatar in full effect. The downside was that the relationships never lasted; how could they? I lived outside myself, not looking into who I was and what I wanted or needed. The truth is, I rarely thought about it.

People often compared my sisters and me. "You look EXACTLY alike! Do you read each other's minds? (yes, pretty much), do you have your own language? (definitely). How come her hair is curlier, she has a freckle, and she is a little bigger or smaller…. you get the picture. It was normalized to be compared. I GET WHY TWINS AND MULTIPLES SEPARATE! But we were connected and made the *UNconscious* agreement to stick it out together through thick and thin. We didn't plan it, but that is how it went year by year.

At 24, we opened our first restaurant and music venue, which would be a wild ride for the next 20 years of incredible highs and lows. We celebrated the great successes, and there were also the epic fights that left me feeling the lowest of the low. We were getting older and looking for more individuality, so we lashed out and pushed and pulled with our restaurants, a very demanding business, as the backdrop. Holy moly, I am glad we survived it.

And then the husbands arrived. Jessica got married, and then Jennifer, both in our early thirties. I was still falling for the "wrong men," I told myself. What was really happening was that my retrofitting and people-pleasing ways would never work. It wasn't the men, it was me. I needed to look within to find my own inner compass, to get clear on what I wanted instead of worrying about what everyone else thought of me. It was years of loneliness, a feeling I had never experienced before. I was hard on myself when I had the realization that I had brought this all on myself. I had been meditating and doing yoga for 20 years, but I had never really looked under this hood of who I REALLY was on my own, without my sisters. When I did, it was pretty much a 5-year dark night of the soul. I would go out with friends and drink too much to fill a void or have dinner for one at home and then walk around the neighborhood and see all the young families doing life together. Both situations left me with a deep pit in my stomach like I was missing out.

Then, it was enough. I decided to pick up my bootstraps. I incorporated more self-love and dug in to get clear on what I wanted my life to look like. I started to travel solo, first on road trips, then out of the country, which was such an edge. I had never traveled alone. In these edgy parts, I found myself. I practiced loving myself despite it all.

At the age of 42, I began again. I became a dance instructor, choreographer, somatic therapy coach, and breathwork facilitator. I started to blend all of these modalities together to teach, lead, and learn in new ways. I love working with groups and continuing to build community, as I did throughout the restaurant years. What I now realize through working with others is that it isn't just multiples that feel this way or middle children, but instead, so many of us who have been programmed to do or think in a certain way have taken on someone else's belief systems and then at some point say, "but wait, what do I want? Who am I? What is my true purpose?" I believe it is the quest of the human experience.

After 25 years, we decided to end the restaurant era and move on to new horizons. My sis Jessica and I created Shine Living Community. We have made the very conscious agreement to do it in a way where both of us have our wings spread wide, and we get to be exactly who we are, unique from one another, and the power we create together. Our other sister set off on her own path, and the switch-up has been incredible for our relationship.

Oh, and the guy….. He came in as soon as I found self-love and comfort in being alone instead of lonely. The moment I looked into his eyes, I knew I found home. I am forever grateful for my entire journey that is still unfolding because it got me where I am today, in my wholeness and still learning and growing.

In moments of challenge, I find things that bring me joy, like putting on a song I love and dancing around the living room, hiking in nature, and even sitting with a tree and speaking to it like an old friend, can be so healing. Or I meet up with a girlfriend, one where you can really let it all hang out and go for tea or a glass of wine. I do something to raise my joy meter instead of staying stuck in a funk. I keep coming back to the words, "Change my energy, change my life." It has been HUGELY helpful. Life is an INside job, after all.

Some sage advice from my experience: Take time to turn the focus inward to you. This isn't selfish; it is necessary. Knowing yourself is true empowerment, and it gives you an incredible inner compass in which to guide your life. Get curious about who you are at your core, your true essence. You are a work of art, a masterpiece that is ever-evolving, and you are unique to any other soul. So meet this miracle of this life with an open heart. The world needs you in all of your authentic glory. You got this.

Jill Emich

Karen Whelan

Spiritual Resilience "You wander from room to room hunting for the diamond necklace that is already around your neck." –Rumi.

I spent a lot of my time searching for myself in others only to discover I was the one I had been waiting for that I was the answer to my problems and the medicine to my pain. Resilience was not a conscious choice; it was a way of being for me from a young age. I grew up in an environment where I endured abuse - both sexual and physical. An environment in which I felt unloved, unlovable, and unwanted.

Remember, you have one life, one chance here to live fearlessly. The path you choose will come down to your relationship with yourself. Come home, come home to you, and greet yourself with love and compassion and let the Divine in.

This manifested as emotional abandonment wounds. Wounds that tested my mental and emotional stability.

The kind of resilience I had to draw upon was based on finding Karen to reclaim my true sense of self that was wounded by inner negative wounds, sabotaging programs, and negative self-image.

Unbecoming to become...

At the tender age of 14, I had become so ferocious in hating Karen that I attempted suicide. The need to not be her devoured me from the inside. I turned to drugs and became homeless, sometimes sleeping on a friend's sofa to dropping out of school at 15. I also turned my back on the Divine as I felt the Divine abandoned me, too.

When you self-hate, you are hating the Divine spark within you. When you turn your back on yourself, you close the door on the Divine. This was the spiritual pain I faced, finding the Divine and recognizing that the Divine was always in my life, especially in the darkest moments. Today, I can affirm connection to the Divine is a deep loving connection and acceptance of who you are. So, I had to find Karen to find the Divine.

I have experienced the transcendental moments of my life. My first experience of transcendence was loving and calm, then self-hate consumed me, and I would feel detached from feeling connected to anything. Yet, the divine was always communicating, even in the chaos. In the chaos, I was looking out at the world from my woundedness – a distorted lens – so I could not receive the messages from the Divine. The dance between unseeing to seeing, from unconscious living to conscious living. A tortured soul who, when in the dark night of the soul, found a way when there was no way to alchemize the darkness into redemption and love.

I began a quest to seek external validation from others and needed material objects just to feel like somebody in society. The irony was by looking outward, I was taking myself further away from home - the embodied self. I was separating from the wisdom within, and chaos became the perfect storm to hide from myself.

I believe in this separation; the Divine was seeking me. This style of communication was to send in lessons through events and people. Messengers gave me what I needed to unbecome the wounded self so I could return home to the self within.

The inner shift came when I let go of the need to be seen and accepted by others. Today, the springboard from which my heart soars is held in a narrative, "you are here for something great. A quest. A soul's mission. This mission is for you to wake up to the truth of who you are. To awaken to who you are truly designed to be upon discovering a profound love within. Being here is your birthright, your inheritance from God".

How do we get to a place of total inner liberation where there is great freedom to be who you are meant to be?

Here are my best tips for reclaiming inner liberation.

Your only job is to self-permit, to give yourself permission to express yourself in whatever way you want. To self-permit in saying yes to life because it's not about what others think. Your story inside of you about what you think others are thinking is a prison cell!

Develop Self-love. This is the component of unshackling your inner limited narratives.

Grow a confident self-image. Remember, nobody can hear the story you tell yourself about yourself, so tell yourself an epic one!

Gratitude: cultivating a mindset of gratitude helps you move from limitation to expansion. Each day, journal what you are grateful for.

Remember, you have one life, one chance here to live fearlessly. The path you choose will come down to your relationship with yourself. Come home, come home to you, and greet yourself with love and compassion and let the Divine in.

Karen Whelan

Kelli Melissa Reinhardt

I lost my middle sister, Carrie, who died by suicide on February 20, 2017, and my son had his 2nd episode of seizures on the day of my sister's celebration of life.

February 20th and 25th, 2017, are two days that will be etched into my mind for eternity...

I was sitting at my desk at work when my mom called. She never called me when she knew I was working. I knew something was wrong at that moment, but I let it go to voicemail because I was on a call with a customer.

A visual voicemail popped up with her message...

"Kelli, it's mom. Call me back". I could tell in the tone something was wrong, and I needed to call her back as soon as possible. I hurried up my call with the customer and called her back.

She was crying very hard, and all she could get out was, "Something very bad happened to Carrie. She is dead."

"Wait, what? What do you mean she is dead?" I responded.

"She hurt herself," my mom responded. "We are on the way back from the cabin and will be there soon."

I couldn't even process what my mom had just said. I don't even know what came out of my mouth after that, but I know I started crying.

I collected myself and went back onto the sales floor.

As I approached my desk, my manager could tell something was wrong. She called me over to her desk and asked what happened.

I lost it and started crying. Through the tears, I was able to tell her. She told me to log out and go.

I felt completely numb, but I went into action mode. I knew I needed to get over to my sister's house before my mom did because, for whatever reason, I thought I needed to be the strong one and didn't want my mom to have to deal with the aftermath.

I'm the youngest of five sisters, and Carrie was one of my middle sisters, so having to be the strong one for everyone was a new thought process for me.

I left work and went straight to my sister's apartment. My son was in daycare, and I had several hours before I had to pick him up. Being at her apartment was surreal.

> It's okay to ask for help. You are not alone. Find a community of incredible people who lift you up, are supportive, and create a safe space for healing.

My nephew and mom showed up a bit after I did, making it even harder. My heart was hurting for my nephew because now he must watch this scene and go through his life without his mom, who he relied on so much. It felt unreal.

Until the coroner rolled her body out of the apartment, then it became more real. I couldn't help but think I wanted to check under the sheet and make sure it was her.

During that same day, the word got out that my sister had passed. One very influential person posted "RIP Carrie" on Facebook, and it was blowing up faster than I could contain. It wasn't even an hour after I watched the coroner roll my sister's body out of the apartment. How did anyone know?!?!

I had to do some damage control because one little person didn't know yet...

My sister's daughter, who was 11 at the time.

We didn't want it to get back to her before we could tell her as a family. I had to reach out to that person and ask them to take down their post, which they gladly did. However, the word was already out. Our phones and messengers started blowing up. I had to put my phone away and turn off alerts because it became too much. Ultimately, I put out a post to alert the masses of friends that it was true my sister had passed.

I remember not wanting to tell anyone that she had died by suicide. It didn't feel like it was anyone's business, and I didn't want anyone to know that was how it happened due to the stigma.

A couple of days later, I finally got my answer as to whether it was truly her beneath that sheet during the viewing, where my mom, other sister, niece, and I were present for our private gathering to give my niece a chance to say goodbye.

At that moment, it was real. She was really gone.

My sister was cremated, and we had her celebration of life five days later.

On the morning of February 25, 2017, I woke up and was about to get ready, and my one-and-a-half-year-old son had a seizure. This was his 2nd episode of seizures in 6 months.

My stepdaughter was running around with my son playing, and suddenly, I heard her and my boyfriend yelling for me. My son was on my stepdaughter's floor right by the door, his eyes rolling into his head, seizing.

"Call 911," I yelled.

Luckily, we live right down the street from a firehouse. The next thing I knew, I heard the sirens and the firefighters tromping up the stairs toward me as I sat next to my son, making sure he was breathing.

They scooped up his limp body and took him down the stairs towards the ambulance. I jumped in, and we headed towards Children's Hospital.

My stepdaughter and boyfriend followed the ambulance in the Jeep.

We arrived at Children's Hospital, and they rushed him into the ER and put us in this oddly shaped room where he had two more seizures, three in all, in a 3-hour span.

The first episode of seizures, six months prior, he had six seizures in 8 hours, and my sister Carrie was there to help guide me and keep me calm. It wasn't fair that she wasn't there this time. She was supposed to be there.

It seemed like divine intervention because my son stopped having seizures, and they moved us to a hospital room just in time for me to leave and go to my sister's celebration of life.

Luckily, my boyfriend, now husband, and his daughter were there too, so they were able to stay at the hospital with my son.

I changed quickly, spoke at my sister's celebration of life, and headed back to the hospital to stay in the NICU with my son overnight.

The following year was pretty much a blur, and my coping mechanism was to keep going, stay busy, and not think about my grief. I had to be strong for my family and my son. It wasn't until I hit a virtual brick wall that I had to finally take care of myself, talk to a therapist, and take some time off work.

I was introduced to Neuro-Linguistic Programming (NLP) through my healing journey. I found forgiveness for my sister and myself, which I never knew I needed. It was life-transforming. Through NLP, I learned how to take care of myself so that I could take care of others.

A year after these two events, I started a mental health and suicide awareness nonprofit called BCC Evolution. We empower humans by providing the knowledge and skills necessary for navigating difficult conversations about mental health, substance abuse, and suicide because education and conversation saves lives!

It's okay to ask for help. You are not alone. Find a community of incredible people who lift you up, are supportive, and create a safe space for healing. If you can't find one, come join ours.

Kelli Melissa Reinhardt

Kelly Chashai

You are not what happened to you but
what you choose to become.

As a human being, I recognized
the beauty in relying solely on our
incredible selves to navigate this
extraordinary life.In this solitude,
I discovered resilience, strength, and
the power to overcome even the darkest
moments.

At the age of 13, tragedy struck my world. The sun shone brightly at the ballpark, marking the last game of the season. Excitement filled the air as I eagerly scanned the stands, searching for the familiar faces of my parents. "Where are they?" I wondered. However, the game ended, and I found myself alone on the diamond, waiting. My optimism faded as a police car pulled up, forever altering the course of my life.

I was escorted to my aunt's house without any clear explanation. Confusion and shock enveloped me during those early moments. Hours passed in a blur, and I suddenly found myself at my home, 13 miles from my aunt's. The realization struck me as I noticed my pants were damp with cold urine – a physical manifestation of the overwhelming emotional turmoil within.

The funeral that followed was a grand affair, attended by both familiar and unfamiliar faces. Navigating through the sea of condolences was bewildering. Should I sit, stand, cry, run, scream, or laugh? My body and mind were out of sync, leaving me floating above the unfolding scenario. Every sympathetic gaze etched with pity intensified the pain; it was undoubtedly the darkest moment of my life.

People often say that time heals all wounds. In my case, time merely cloaked the wounds with a scab, allowing me to soldier on. The days that followed were a precarious dance with uncertainty. Where would I go? What would become of me? Who would be my family now?

Relocating to a new city, I found myself in the confines of a family not my own. The basement bedroom became my refuge, and periodic visits to the "upstairs family" revealed a world of strange rules, unwritten norms, and complex power dynamics. I documented the intricacies as an observer, eventually channeling my observations into a novel-like ledger. Each day, I crafted happy endings for myself, creating a parallel reality that provided solace and a tether to my identity.

My unconventional pre-13 life, with its nomadic undertones, served as my foundation for survival. The interactions and conversations I absorbed during those formative years prepared me for this life-altering moment. Even as an only child in an adult world, I embraced the nomadic lifestyle as it was my university.

Throughout the tumultuous journey, I held the belief that I only had myself. As a human being, I recognized the beauty in relying solely on our incredible selves to navigate this extraordinary life.In this solitude, I discovered resilience, strength, and the power to overcome even the darkest moments.

Kelly Chashai

Kera Sanchez

I found out my mother died on vacation in Italy while I was in the NICU with my newborn.

Ironically, I rediscovered my love for writing when the words of my mom's obituary flowed out of me. It was easy to do, honestly. She lived a very full, vibrant, impactful, yet short life, making it all the more effortless, minus the gaping hole she left in my life.

Just days before receiving the earth-shattering call, my mother had been at the hospital with me when my youngest daughter was born, as a strange set of circumstances allowed her to be present and to meet her newest grandchild. A weekend in late May designed to honor our fallen and reserved for BBQs and excited conversations about summer plans is where my story begins. I was eight months pregnant with a fever and chills. After avoiding the illness that shall not be named for nearly two years, it finally caught up to me. Within the subsequent 48 hours, I felt better, but the shooting pains of labor were also added to the mix. I had previously given birth at 37 weeks with my first, but this time, an entire month would be eliminated from my gestational period. My husband and I decided it was time to call the hospital.

My OB already knew I had COVID, and when discussing my admission to the hospital, it didn't seem like my pesky viral friend would be an issue, yet on the way, they called me back to inform me of the Hospital policies. I would be admitted, and once my labor was confirmed, they would allow my husband, Mike, to join me. After changing into the glamorous, ass-less gown, I was pacing my room for what felt like an eternity, and the nurse finally returned.

"I'm sorry, but since your husband also had COVID, we can't allow him up. Is there someone who could accompany you who is COVID-free?"

My mind started to spiral, and I was too panicked to be angry. My birth plan quickly started to play second fiddle as I was faced with the terror of having to do this alone, without my husband. The contractions started up again, and I could barely respond. Once they dissipated, I called my husband in a frenzy. "They won't let you up. They said no! I have to do this alone or find someone who doesn't have COVID to accompany me." He said he would call me back and to hold tight.

Normally, calling my mom would have been a no-brainer, but we were in a weird spot in our relationship. We recently had been arguing a lot and not seeing eye to eye on things that now don't matter nor affect my love for her and the love we shared for 34 years prior. Plus, she was getting ready to leave on a two-week European voyage with 30 friends through Italy and Greece.

A piece of advice I would love to leave you with is to find a positive community and others who understand your pain. I also encourage anyone to allow the grief to change them. Not in a negative way but to look for ways in which it has opened new windows and understandings about life. Death is the master teacher to learn about life and what we want to achieve on borrowed time. Lean in and lean often.

After a few minutes, my phone started to buzz, and I answered my tearful husband, who was devastated by the realization that he would not be present for our daughter's birth and also scared for his wife, who was currently sitting alone in her pain. "Sweetie, listen to me; your mom is on her way. She will be there within the hour. You can do this, baby, you got this."

While I was mourning our situation, I also instantly felt relief. At that exact moment, I was simply a girl who needed her mom. If my husband couldn't be there, that was the next best thing, regardless of our relational state.

Witnessing my mom burst into the room in her black waffle hoodie felt like the comfort I craved at that juncture. We hugged so tight, and we both expressed how sorry we were for the past and the arguments that didn't seem to carry weight in the present. I vividly remember my mom telling me, "I don't want to fight with you ever again." It felt like such a sacred and magical moment in time that would be the first step in repairing our relationship. I was hopeful and excited for the months to come, to make up for lost time, for her to come home from her vacation rested, with souvenirs for her grandkids and the memories we would make.

The reality is we never did fight again because less than a week later, her life was cut short at the age of 57. Two days into her trip while in Naples, Italy, the ambulance that was called arrived too late.

Sitting in the NICU nursery with the bliss of motherhood and bonding with the baby I could finally hold, I received the call. I'm certain the nurses will still tell you the blood-curdling scream that I released was far more disturbing than any woman in labor they have heard throughout the years. I had just lived a lifetime high, followed by an immediate lifetime low.

So I sit, days after the birth of my daughter and the death of my mother, writing an obituary filled with stories of inspiration, hard work, adventure, laughs, and a life well lived that was cut far too short. Much like her stature, my mom was a bigger-than-life personality in a bite-size figure. J, as many students and friends affectionately called her throughout the years, was a nickname taken from the first letter of her last name, Jacobson. She was sparkly, funny, bold, blunt, loud, mischievous, the life of the party, and she had just completed an Irish exit that no one expected.

In the time that followed, postpartum depression and the immense grief I experienced from the loss of the mother I so badly needed were braided together during my maternity leave. For months, I ruminated on many things. Life, death, and why this had happened to me and to my children, who will now grow up without either of their grandmothers. (My mother-in-law had also passed away about a year prior from Cancer)

Another rumination was how, one day, my daughters would experience this pain and this loss when I die. It was such a disturbing thought as I was rocking my newborn. It was then that I had an instantaneous thought, a spark, an idea, and a solution: a guided journal that would walk us through all the things we need to leave our loved ones. A guided journal of love, advice, and support to leave our own. As a teacher, I have a creative brain, and it's in my wheelhouse to think of a complex topic such as this and break it down into bite-sized, manageable pieces. I wrote half of my guided journal that day and spent the next three months perfecting it. I leveraged that grief into a tool that could help others, "Legacy Letters Guided Journal," and months later, "No Legacy Lost," yet another guided journal for grievers—a place to keep memories of our loved ones safely. I envisioned journaling about my mom and mother-in-law, and my daughters would one day pull that book from the shelf and be able to read more about their beautiful grandmothers, robbed of their experience of spoiling and loving their grandchildren.

While advertising for my book, my Instagram page slowly grew from a platform to talk about my journals to a place to document my grief journey. I created grief content and took my life back, one dark, humorous reel at a time. I inherited my bigger-than-life personality from my mom, and I felt like that personality was robbed for a while. Being able to openly talk about my grief on Instagram, my way, with my humor, I began to feel myself come back to my body. I felt like grief controlled me for months, but now, I was controlling the grief and my story. I also began to host Instagram LIVE interviews with other members of the grief community. I realized there was a common thread: grief was a conduit to creativity and inspirational stories.

Again, my teacher's brain kicked in. I know how important community and recognition are to thrive and heal, and I had another spark of creativity: a magazine. A magazine that would amplify the voices of grievers everywhere. A place to highlight inspiring stories of loss, a place to learn from experts and peers, and a place that would serve as a creative outlet for all members of the grief community to share their stories, as well as poetry, writing, art, photography, recipes, and more.

Since the loss of my mother, I have learned a lot about death but even more about life, and that is what I am doing. Creating community and resources for people living with loss who still have life left to live, a legacy to leave, and a story to share.

Practicing resilience was one step at a time. I allowed the hardest parts of life to break me, but I also allowed the sun to touch upon those cracks and jagged pieces, and it was healing. I found that while sharing my story with others, every time I voiced what happened to me, I gained more confidence and control over the narrative I was sharing, and I noticed the same about others. That radiated love, and while sharing these terrible experiences with others, I was also seeing the good they do, and it creates hope and inspiration for the future.

A piece of advice I would love to leave you with is to find a positive community and others who understand your pain. I also encourage anyone to allow the grief to change them. Not in a negative way but to look for ways in which it has opened new windows and understandings about life. Death is the master teacher to learn about life and what we want to achieve on borrowed time. Lean in and lean often.

Kera Sanchez

Krista Neill

As far back as I can remember, being a mother was always my heart's deepest desire. I may not have realized it then, but from an early age, I started making *big life* decisions based on the unquestioned belief that I would someday have a *little life* to love and call my own. Being a mother was so embedded in my future identity that planning and preparing for my one-day baby was the fuel to my life's fire.

When the day did come to start trying for my long-awaited baby, I was well aware that my biological clock was ticking but, I found reassurance in celebrity news headlines that I was well within the normal age range to miraculously get pregnant. However, after several months of negative pregnancy tests, it became increasingly obvious that I was not going to be as lucky as those who graced the glossy magazine covers and so, I sought professional advice. At that time, I still felt extremely optimistic, believing that it was only a matter of time before my long-awaited dream of being a mom would come true. Surely, hope, love, and a little bit of science would be the magic ingredients I needed.

It wasn't until I was sitting at the desk of my third fertility doctor that doubt started to creep in. After reviewing my file, which was now over three years deep with disappointments, he looked up at me and asked, "What defines motherhood to you?" At that moment, I knew the truth that he was cradling in his question, but I was not yet ready to accept it. At that time, not being able to have a biological child was an unfathomable thought because, for me, a life without that little bundle of DNA was not a life worth living. Thus, despite the implanted seed of hopelessness, I was not prepared to give up on the only dream I had ever had. Instead, I went into overdrive getting my name on the waitlists of the best fertility doctors with the highest success rates, abundantly devouring fertility-boosting foods and supplements, booking weekly appointments with every type of healing practitioner imaginable, trying new non-toxic lotions and potions, as well as altering any other variable that I could think of in a desperate attempt to control the forewarned outcome.

My advice for anyone else facing infertility challenges or living a childless-not-by-choice life is to be vulnerable, honour your feelings, and speak your truth. Know that you do not have to suffer in silence. Create a network of people who can help support you.

My endeavours took me to multiple clinics across North America, exploring various avenues to motherhood and enduring countless pokes, prods, and procedures until a melanoma diagnosis put a (temporary) pause on my pursuit. Thankfully, I caught the cancer at an early stage and underwent a successful removal; however, the news post-surgery was not all positive. My doctors informed me that not only was there emerging evidence regarding the correlation between melanoma and estrogen but that melanoma is one of the few forms of cancer that can cross the placenta during pregnancy.

Balancing my desire for motherhood with the need to prioritize both my health and the health of my future baby became an intricate dance of emotions and decisions. The differing opinions I was given about the statistics and probabilities of comparable cases added to my twirling thoughts of *Should I or shouldn't I?* Although I so desperately wanted to deny the truth that was once again being delivered to me, I knew the choice I had to make. I stopped all attempts at becoming pregnant because, to me, a motherless child is far more tragic than a childless woman. Not willing to give up entirely on being a mom, I spent the following years exploring other avenues to motherhood, including surrogacy, third-party reproduction, and the possibility of adoption. As I feared, those years were filled with more heartbreak, disappointments, tough decisions, and hard truths, which finally pushed me to my breaking point. I no longer recognized myself as the years of my relentless pursuit of motherhood had finally caught up to me. I knew that to save myself, I had to step back, re-evaluate the meaning of life, and begin to mourn the death of my dream.

Letting go of the life I had meticulously curated in my mind required strength I never knew I had. The resiliency that I needed to endure the seven years of various forms of fertility treatments was just the beginning because although I had decided to stop trying for a baby physically, the emotional yearning never resigned.

What many people do not realize is that infertility gives you a lifetime membership to a club you never asked to be a part of. A club that puts your life on hold for years, one that tests all of your relationships, makes you second guess your purpose, doubt your self-worth, and shatters your self-esteem. For those of us who are never promoted to the exclusive #MomClub, we are left with a permanent, invisible wound that reopens with every pregnancy announcement, diaper commercial, baby shower invitation, or the subsequent kids' birthday parties that we (and our non-existent child) never get invited to but see on social media. Girls' nights become playdates, catch-up conversations revolve around daycare dilemmas and commonalities with dear friends start to disappear.

As the years march on and the stages of life change, so does the nature of the daily reminders. The 'birth announcement babies' turn into the 'kindergarten graduate kids' who will continue to be the reminding sources that I will never get to witness *my* child reaching life milestones, celebrate holidays with, or become a grandma. Thus, although the passage of time does help in some ways, there will always be little pokes that will reopen the wound that will never fully heal. My story of resiliency is learning how to live a happy and fulfilling life despite this.

Almost a decade since my journey began, resiliency continues to be a daily practice for me. It is grounded in radical acceptance, which allows me the grace to still have sad days, to feel sorry for myself, to miss and yearn for the life I once dreamt of, *and* to be happy and grateful for the life I do have. I now prioritize self-love, set boundaries around triggering situations, seek opportunities that bring me joy, and put my energy and attention into things I can control. I regularly set new, fluid life goals and have shifted my focus from *creating a life* to *creating a life that I love.* In doing this, I have learned that painful challenges can be transformed into opportunities for growth and empowerment.

For me, this meant leaving behind a teaching career and becoming a clinical counselor specializing in relational living, couples counseling, and infertility support. Turning pain into purpose has helped me heal by helping others and trying to make sense of a situation I do not fully understand. And even though I stopped looking for motherhood a few years ago, I keep my heart open that one day it will find me; it might just look different than what I had always imagined it to be.

Looking back at my journey, I realize what a pivotal moment it was when the doctor asked me that question so many years ago; a source of doubt then has become my source of hope now. As I travel down this unexpected path of life, I am hopeful for the opportunities still awaiting me as I continue to learn and redefine not only myself but also what motherhood means to me.

My advice for anyone else facing infertility challenges or living a childless-not-by-choice life is to be vulnerable, honour your feelings, and speak your truth. Know that you do not have to suffer in silence. Create a network of people who can help support you. During my years of treatments, I found other women on Instagram who were also experiencing fertility challenges who knew exactly what I was going through. Having this emotional camaraderie of empathetic support not only helped me but inspired my career change. My online sisterhood of warriors (as we liked to call ourselves) taught me the power of story-sharing and made me feel less alone and broken during what was arguably the most challenging time of my life. To this day, some of those women continue to be dear friends of mine. Also, learn how to set boundaries to protect your heart and, perhaps most importantly, do not compare yourself or your journey with others. We all have our own paths to walk in this lifetime; embrace yours and love yourself no matter what. Fertility does not define you.

Krista Neill

Lainie Rosner

After losing my mother to breast cancer when I was 20, I grew up expecting to get cancer eventually. It did finally happen, but not in the way I anticipated.

Lots of forest bathing and exercise helped me breathe through the stress. A supportive family, community, and memories of the strong women I came from helped me cope.

I learned resilience from an early age. My parents were teachers; my grandparents were Holocaust survivors. I was a competitive gymnast surrounded by role models who taught me to be thankful, challenge myself, breathe through stress, and approach life with bravery and determination. I learned the importance of independence, family, and community to celebrate life.

My mom died of breast cancer at 49. I was 20. Because she was diagnosed at 32, I started mammograms in my 20s. I wanted to catch any lumps early when (not if) they came. The decision to go on the pill was a conundrum for me as it increases breast cancer risk.

I embraced opportunities that came my way in education, sport, dance, art, and adventure. One of my mom's favorite sayings, "Enjoy life; it's not a dress rehearsal," guided me.

Time, yoga, and counseling helped me address my fear of dying young. I married at 39, and shortly after, we decided to start a family, but things didn't go as planned. Luckily, we had the resources to explore our options.

We did one round of IVF in 2019 and learned on New Year's Eve that none of the embryos were euploid. Devastated, we opted to try again, which resulted in one normal embryo. We were thrilled yet terrified that we had only one chance at this. We started preparing my body for the embryo transfer with a cocktail of hormones. An optional uterine receptivity test was offered, which we did for the best chance of success. I received an endometrial cancer diagnosis instead. Not breast or ovarian cancer, which I had always expected, but in my uterus, which was never a concern. In one moment, our world pivoted from creating new life to fear of the worst. Thankfully, the pathology report determined that the cancer was treatable. We shared our news with our circle, and amazingly, my dear friend Cheryl unhesitatingly offered to be our surrogate. The week before the scheduled transfer into Cheryl, we learned that my cancer was now high-grade and surgery was urgent.

Within a few weeks, medical technology would implant my embryo into my friend to grow into a viable baby and laparoscopically remove my reproductive system so I could live to see that baby grow up. As COVID restrictions eased, I attended Cheryl's OB-GYN appointments. It was surreal to watch the dancing patterns on the monitor that was my baby inside C and a strange juxtaposition to be at the same hospital where I met with my oncologist.

Lots of forest bathing and exercise helped me breathe through the stress. A supportive family, community, and memories of the strong women I came from helped me cope.

My husband, Cheryl's husband, and I were all present when our miracle baby girl was born in July 2022.

Lainie Rosner

Leah Kaplan

I remember the first day of school like it was yesterday.

All these years later, I still advise children in difficult family situations - to find people they can rely on for support, whether friends or other relatives. No child should have to feel alone in the world.

I was only five years old, but my birthday was in December, so I was one of the youngest in my class. Our house was just a ten-block walk from the school, but it felt like miles to a little five-year-old like me.

All the other kids had their mothers walk them to school that morning, but my mother worked long hours at her dress shop, so the caregivers were responsible for getting me ready. I was so nervous walking those few blocks alone, clutching my little lunch bag tightly. When I finally reached the classroom, the teacher directed us all to our assigned seats. That's when it happened - I was so scared and overwhelmed that I had an accident right there at my desk.

The other kids must have noticed, but at least the teacher was kind about it. Still, I was mortified. When I got home that afternoon, the caregiver was furious with me. "You're a big girl now. You don't wet your pants!" she scolded. Her harsh words only made me feel worse.

I just wanted my mother to comfort me, but she was never home except for Sundays.

Those early school years were lonely without my mom. I would call her shop in tears, begging her to come home. On the weekends, she was exhausted from working all week, so we didn't get to spend much quality time together either. My brothers and I shared a small bedroom in our cramped house, while my parents had their own room. I slept in a crib until I was eight years old.

Everything changed when we moved to a bigger house with more bedrooms. I finally got my own bed - it felt like such a luxury! But the best part was when my Zaida moved in after my grandmother passed away. Zaida doted on me and became the parent I so desperately needed. Every afternoon, he would make me a snack, and we would play games together. Those moments with Zaida are some of my happiest childhood memories.

Looking back, I can see how much being raised without my mother impacted me as an adult. I chose to be a stay-at-home mom for my kids so that they would never feel as lonely and neglected as I did. All these years later, I still advise children in difficult family situations - to find people they can rely on for support, whether friends or other relatives. No child should have to feel alone in the world.

Leah Kaplan

Linda Giangreco

The diary of a stupid new girl.

It was my sixth elementary school in five years in three different Southern California towns by the age of 9. I'm not sure how I wound up in this one, but I knew I felt differently about it, not in a good way. It was the third day of the week, Wednesday, and I knew what that meant: the dreaded reading circle.

Five tables of five children each meant to provide a public display of their reading

expertise aloud to the entire classroom, one by one. One paragraph each.

The experience of physical and mental terror that ran through my entire body every Wednesday at noon at the lunch table was palpable. Any packed lunch in my pink metal Barbie lunchbox became inedible and nauseating no matter how much love it was packed with.

My expectation of what was coming next, amplified by my consistent inability to focus and be in the present moment, was made even worse than the usual terrifying things, like being the only new kid in class again and akin to my parents arguing and threatening and throwing accusations like cars flying by on a fast California freeway.

The bell rang, and I hesitated, basically frozen on the cold Formica cafeteria bench. Palms sweating, not wanting to be ushered out by the lunch monitor, I picked up my thermos, placed it in my lunchbox, and then dumped its entire contents into the trash and slowly walked to get into the line to enter my fourth-grade classroom. It would be the fifth thermos my parents would have to replace by mid-year.

Good fortune did look down on me, though. Situated alphabetically, the young boy who sat immediately next to me, Gregg, with two "Gs," he announced to me, was an excellent reader. Whether he took pity on me or he was just a sweet-hearted boy (I would find out later in high school when we became close friends, that it was the latter), he helped me to try to get the words right by whispering them to me when he sensed I was struggling and continued even when the teacher admonished him for it.

By the end of the school year, things were not much better.

The oddly intoxicating scent of freshly pumped gasoline from the back seat of my folks T-bird didn't make the drive back and forth between Palm Springs and LA to my grandmother's home any less arduous. It was done every other week once my grandfather had passed. One of the tasks my parents gave me was to attempt to read the sun-bleached billboards that dotted the side of the freeway.

You may have found yourself struggling in areas of your life that others seemingly breeze through. Please give yourself the grace of remembering that we are each unique humans with 'unique to us' gifts to bring to our families and the world at large.

Your struggles make you hungry for access to the things you think your weak spots keep you from, but those same inabilities are actually your Super Powers. They call you forth to be creative, try harder, and bring your successes to fruition because you never ever give up.

I would sound the words out carefully, but I could not connect the letters to the sounds and the sounds to all the grammatical rules I had been taught from the various schools I attended. Each attempt to connect the dots seemed to end in disappointment until one entirely too long trip back home. Approaching the offramp that would lead them into Palm Springs and away from any remaining faded signage, I gave it one more chance. I attempted to reread a billboard that I had tried to read fifty times before as they sped by, pronouncing each word to myself quietly from the back seat:

PALl-um sp-ringsS-Pā

Pallmm Springs S-p-ahhh, I said a bit louder. Palm Springs Spa, I said (having no idea what spa meant), then cautiously and confidently said it again so my parents could hear, "Palm Springs Spa!" My mom and stepdad mouthed each word with me as I repeated it. My stepdad was truly giddy, and my mom was thrilled. "You did it, you did it, they said, and I exclaimed, "I can! I can read, I can read, I can read!

From that point forward, the reading floodgates opened. Slowly, I moved on to reading books that were more interesting to me. I tried to teach myself the languages of all the places I wanted to go and read recipes for all the treats I wanted to make. I became a voracious reader, not necessarily a great student, but a really good cook: Ya win some, ya lose some. I did become a successful entrepreneur in various types of businesses, and they say people have genius for what they are passionate about. I was passionate about many things, especially never being considered the stupid new girl in school again. Reading meant I had access to everything I could imagine and everything I couldn't.

I never gave up trying to read. It meant I would be "normal, " fit in, and be accepted by my new peers. It would mean I wasn't stupid and a disappointment to my family. Basically, it was everything.

My initial inability to read was a function of a learning difference that, at the time, went undiagnosed. I learn differently and understand things deeply. You may have found yourself struggling in areas of your life that others seemingly breeze through. Please give yourself the grace of remembering that we are each unique humans with 'unique to us' gifts to bring to our families and the world at large.

Your struggles make you hungry for access to the things you think your weak spots keep you from, but those same inabilities are actually your Super Powers. They call you forth to be creative, try harder, and bring your successes to fruition because you never ever give up.

Linda Giangreco

Lori Frazier

I was pregnant with my last child (son). I was at risk of losing him. I had high blood pressure, I had placenta Pre-via, and I was overweight.

To practice resilience, I talk to myself about the situation, and I pray a lot.

In certain situations, you must do what is right to survive.

I was at work doing inventory. And we were about to get robbed. My son's father was out in the parking lot and discovered that we were about to get robbed. He quickly ran into the facility I was in and told me to come on and leave. I was the manager, and I could not leave the employees. So I immediately ran to the office and notified the police. As I was on the phone with them, I was shaking. Police came and arrested guys, and that's when it hit.

I went into shock. I was bleeding everywhere. I disturbed my pregnancy with nervousness. I was taken to the hospital. That's when I was told I miscarried the one, and he could not be saved. But the other one is still in me and will survive only if I take off work. That means complete bed rest. So, I was willing to cooperate because I did not want to lose my other son. He would have been my one and only son. It was hard to stay on bed rest with two other children (girls at that!) Even though their dad was present, I could not keep still.

Then, the spotting happened. I went to my doctor, who transferred me to the emergency room. I was losing my other son. So, that's when it hit me. I have to do it right. But the doctor has a different idea from me. I was hospitalized for two months until I delivered my son. Even though I was against staying, I stayed. I was so bored at the hospital, but it was best for me. I was eating the right foods, resting, and exercising.

And I did have my son early. He weighed only 1 pound 11 ounces. It was still a scare because of all the symptoms predicted. Yes, I said predicted. But we beat all the odds, and I now have a 24-year-old son who is as healthy as an ox.

To practice resilience, I talk to myself about the situation, and I pray a lot.

In certain situations, you must do what is right to survive.

Take all proper measurements.

Lori Frazier

Martha Kartaoui

I spent twenty-five years in a highly physically, spiritually, sexually, emotionally, and verbally abusive religious cult. The abuse started at age nine.

Our circumstances, trauma, and personal hell may be different, but pain is pain. You feel lonely but are not alone. I see you, I was you! But, there is hope; focus on the small light within. Let it guide you and keep you focused. Healing is a process; it's not always easy, but you are worth it!

Dec 27, 2004, will always be a date in my life that represents courage, hope, strength, and resilience. That day is forever memorialized in my mind as the night that everything changed and I took my life back. It's the night I physically escaped the religious cult that I had been born into. I had been held in the leader's compound for almost eight years prior, and it was my living hell.

I had been praying, plotting, and planning my escape for about ten days. I didn't know how I would manage this feat, but I felt the enormity of my situation in every fiber of my being because my every move was monitored!

Growing up, I didn't know our group was a cult. I thought we were part of a secret society; it was ingrained in us that the outside world was scary, evil, and dangerous, and we were safe because we were the chosen. We were taught that the outside world would not understand our ways, so we didn't talk about it, and if we were questioned, our instinct was to lie.

In 1975, my parents joined the group "The Disciples of the Lord Jesus Christ." The leader, who we now call "cultman," was intertwined in all aspects of our lives. He controlled everything, from what we ate to the children's names, what we wore, what kind of job to take, and where and whether we would go to college. He made every decision for us.

We did not celebrate birthdays, anniversaries, or holidays. No chocolate, coffee, pasta, pizza, pork, tea, candy, soda, alcohol, etc. Rules and rituals changed at cultman's whim, and we never questioned or asked for an explanation.

At age 9, my sexual abuse began. There was so much fear and shame! I wish this were an isolated experience, but it was just the first of many to come within and outside the group. I became a pro at painting on a smile, covering my feelings, and overcompensating by being loud, obnoxious, and outrageous.

Physical abuse at the hands of the cultman started at about age six and was ongoing. The smallest infraction would lead to calculated torture or beatings with 2x4s, metal switches, extension cords, 3ft wooden ladles, cattle prods, storage barrels, basically anything he could get his hands on. Manipulation, brainwashing, and verbal, spiritual, sexual, physical, and emotional abuse are all things that I recognize now were our everyday existence. These things were exercised to keep us controlled, in fear, and isolated.

At age 12, we moved from MN to NC. Families had their own homes, and we traveled each weekend to fellowship and work at the cultman's compound in Northeastern WI, a sprawling 200+ acres. Most families commuted 4-5 hours one way.

Seven days after I graduated high school, I was instructed by cultman to move to the compound. There, I was starved for five months, beaten routinely, many times so severely that I should have had medical attention. I attempted to run away and was caught, resulting in my head being shaved 18 times and all of my possessions burned.

I managed the cult's first public business. I worked seven days a week, 365 days a year, for over four years with zero compensation.

I am ready to live out loud, be my authentic self, and share my truth to bring light, hope, and connection to others with shared experiences! My traumatic past does not define me. Instead, I am resilience, strength, hope, joy, love and healing. I am defined by the supernatural strength I found by reconnecting to SELF.

Our circumstances, trauma, and personal hell may be different, but pain is pain. You feel lonely but are not alone. I see you, I was you! But, there is hope; focus on the small light within. Let it guide you and keep you focused. Healing is a process; it's not always easy, but you are worth it!

Martha Kartaoui

Matthew DeRyckere

I grew up with a physically abusive alcoholic father. This caused me a lot of anger and confusion about how to process my emotions.

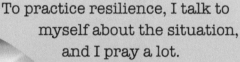

To practice resilience, I talk to myself about the situation, and I pray a lot.

In certain situations, you must do what is right to survive.

In 2000, my father died, and I thought I was free; boy, was I wrong. I started using alcohol as a way to mask my problems and push them down. I immersed myself in the party scene and drank heavily for the next 20 years as a way to cope.

The death of my sister in 2016 was particularly traumatic and sent me into a downward spiral. I drank more and started using cocaine, at first telling myself it wasn't a problem since I wasn't buying it myself. My substance abuse changed who I was as a person, but I didn't realize it at the time since I was in the middle of my addiction.

My marriage was toxic due to my alcoholism. I wasn't fully present, as the drunk version of myself is very different. The death of my sister and the problems in my marriage made my drinking and cocaine use even worse. I blamed my ex-wife for not being supportive enough during this difficult time, but now I understand that I was also unsupportive of myself and others due to my addiction.

In 2019, my wife and I separated. I decided to go on a trip to the Dominican Republic to visit my sister to clear my mind, thinking it would help. However, within a few days, actually a few hours, I was drinking heavily, using cocaine, and making unsafe decisions like buying drugs from strangers in back alleys. During the visit, I was very distracted by my thoughts due to drinking every day. Near the end of the visit for one last night of debauchery, I ended up bringing a sex worker back to my sister's home late at night, which caused a huge confrontation when my family found out.

My sister intervened and had a friend who owned a recovery center speak to me. I broke down in tears, realizing the pain and estrangement I had caused over 20 years. My sister gave me an ultimatum - get sober or be cut off from the family permanently. This was the wake-up call I needed. I attended my first AA meeting that day and have now been sober for over four years.

Since getting sober, I have rebuilt relationships with my family and am in a much better place mentally and emotionally. I have a newfound self-love and can look at myself in the mirror with pride rather than disgust. Quitting drinking allowed me to process my trauma and grief in a healthy way. I now have supportive relationships and offer help to others struggling with addiction to not give up on themselves.

My story shows how addiction is often rooted in past pain and how recovery leads to personal growth.

Matthew DeRyckere

Nana Adu-Boafo Jnr

Resilience of A Brave Sailor

As Ghanaians, there is this expectation to have hard skin against emotional, psychological, and mental challenges, especially after dwelling in the midst of daily hardship and surviving.

So, in an attempt to protect this resilience that we are expected to associate ourselves with, instead of developing it individually, we break people and, worse, force them to be silent about their brokenness.

We tell them to be quiet and "hide away their tears and pains under their armpit.

Some will even tell you, "Don't be depressed; don't ever tell them you are depressed."

My mother, Mrs. Mary Kutin, will say, do remember to hide your pain under your armpit Oooooo....

Ghanaians are never depressed; it is the white man's tea and language... but if you don't have resilience, you will give up easily or even kill yourself!

I was a very young Sailor in the Ghana Navy.

I was pushed through so many traumatic things, bullying, attacks, disrespect, abuse, and bitter experiences like a cockroach in the midst of fowls ...

Like, cockroaches too can dance Oooo...

But because of hens and cocks, cockroaches can't ever end their dance, so I made up my mind to study in the Military rather than worry myself and my head about the troubles they were creating for me.

So I requested to join my trade course. It was officially permitted with plans to worry me the more, but my resilience energy was too strong and harder, like my erections, than their evil thoughts.

I attended my Trade Course on Attachment at Tema Naval Base, and through storms and thrones, I passed all my Military Exams, including the Military Law Exams.

My own people set me up severally.
A lot lied about me,
Which created space for many to hate me.
Luckily, they had no real proof against me on anything. They just hated me and troubled me for nothing.

And I am so happy my positive thoughts and resilience brought me to this point in my life.

Cheers to life, and don't give up yet!

There are better days ahead, so smile, pray, and wait.

Like the Widow's Son, who will offer me help in this jungle I call home?

If families are no longer family to you, who else is blood? Tell me!

The Military system in my Country is sick of something I don't know yet.

Why are most of the younger ones absenting themselves without official leave?

Oh! The poor weary
They live in fury
Weak hope daily
Day and night a day like years
A thousand
Crying out loud
Calling for help
Reasoning beyond imagination

Anticipating a better day to come someday when this sick system of tribal hatred, political hatred, religious hatred, and attacks on individuals with their own beliefs

I have experienced so many bitter things and scenes as a young Sailor. At a point, I agreed with my inner being and spirit to walk out from the Military and focus on my dreams and other abilities.

Alas!

Life of pain
Life of adversity
Hope halt
Appalling day
Horrendous night
A life of fear and fight
All for their right
For their heroes' past
With myopia sightings

Sir Godwin Matey Sackitey once said,

Those Commanders are commanding nothing and are blindfolded with self riches, greed, envy, jealousy, hatred, lies, politics, and tribalism without any righteousness in their intentions...

He said some are even Masons without the squarely conduct and upright behaviors.

Kenneth and Debby will say,
Self-heart and self-centered
Short-sighted of sufferings
And the pain of the people,
Longer sufferings with
Shorter fun.

I have suffered a lot of mentally challenging times and issues, but I am always stronger than my fears.

I am joyfully out of the service now.

I am currently a Stool Chief at Kon, a traditional Ruler of my Community and my forefathers' land.

Ah! Imagine if I committed suicide during those my hardest times, but that never even came to mind.

My mind was to be a better person than the system that was maltreating me.

My mind was to endure all the pains with the resilient spirit of long-suffering, and I made it.

I am a better MAN now, and I can endure every pain and bitter scene because those hardest moments made me the stronger man I am today ...

I am now praying for a NEW Government that will work in the interests of the people and not their stomachs, but unfortunately here,

We always vote for a new government,

I mean,

New government

New pains,

New taxes,

New sufferings, I mean special sufferings that will enter your bones and hit your waist with pains.

In my Country, we have good and fertile lands that can grow everything, and we also have a lot of natural resources, but what is killing us is not diarrhea or cholera but bad Government and greedy Governance.

Our leaders are wearing expensive glasses but still have those old myopia eyes.

Heroes are still falling.
Good people are running and dying prematurely
Praying to halt their adversity
Many were chosen
But few were called

Oh! Oh! Oh! Oh! Ghana, my motherland,

Blair! How long should we hope for change?

Since the days of Dr. Emmanuel Kwadwo Kwarteng Boahen, all they preach is a change that we can't see.

Should I talk of the chaos in my country today,
Let me not speak of the sufferings and injustice today,

If you're not resilient with the spirit of resilience, you will even end up hanging yourself in my Country.

Our leaders are the emissaries of corruption
Yet, in public, they wage war against corruption
They have led us into the jaws of poverty,
Despite our resources, we have drowned in poverty,

Still, I want to stay in Ghana.
For all my life, I'll spend to change Ghana, my motherland, so fret naught, my brothers and sisters. Let's hope for sunshine because there is sun in the sky, so there is hope for a brighter day someday.

May God and His gods
Let the pain and suffering
Be gone forever
As for me, I am not giving up here,

I am still riding my road to reach my destination with my fate and my faith.

Even if they remove my poles, I will still reach my goals in the name of my hometown, Rivers, and gods.

Africa!

Only if we spent the same energy we use in rubbing men's minds with ego could we address the issues that we teach their egos to protect in the first place.

The childhoods of many boys are stifled with this mentality of what it means to "be a man with resilience " in a way that forces most of them to make worse decisions in the face of admitting weakness.

Many without strong minds, dreams, and life plans even commit suicide, and others are also busily building their own suicidal thoughts. Still, I, Nana Adu-Boafo, have healthy and helpful life plans. My joy is to scare whatever scares me and overcome every fear and tear in my circle.

In my mind, I have this stronger and constant reminder that God and my hometown, Rivers, have not forgotten me… so I won't allow any person or anything to break me down or kill me under this shining Sun.

Everyone in life has some sort of strange stories and troubles, and mine is to defeat my troubles and fears to be ME every day...

As Princess Adu-Boafo said:

"When we want experiences, we go to concerts or museums, but when we want the meaningful experience, we go to the storyteller.".. so many blessings, peace, light, healing, and love to my dearest friend Blair Kaplan Venables for knocking my door for my piece of the story too.

Godsway Tek will say storytelling is the best way to express your feelings and the things you faced through which your life has changed.

Storytelling is the easiest way to remember my learning process, and a story described by facts and figures will be remembered for far longer.

Similarly, good stories create a sense of connection, so it is essential to pursue storytelling in your child and enable them to listen to others' stories, through which they could learn some innovative things that will be helpful in their upcoming life!!!!

Continuing my resilience story as a resilient person and character, my temple transforms into a body where the hopeless is now full of hope, and I am not a stranger to my stronger thoughts.

If you're thinking and considering giving up, Trust me, do not do it.

My experiences remind me of many conversations I have had with several women who have experienced one form of intense emotional pain inflicted by someone else.

What is fascinating is how women tend to feed their perpetrator's lack of conscience while swallowing responsibilities, blame, and shame that does not belong to them.

Please be strong to endure and to overcome every obstacle in your life, don't commit suicide, and don't consider any suicidal thoughts into reality.

Be strong and be focused on something because when you're not serious in life, life will take its focus away from you ....

I am my backbone, and my mind is stronger than my fears and tears ...

I have fought too much as a soldier.

I have crossed all the Rivers of pains and rejections.

I have been through a lot that a pen of even a poet cannot poem.

I have suffered a lot of humiliating scenes.

I mean,

Too much sweat,
Too many false allegations and blackmail,
Too much hatred and envy,
Too many hours of heated problems and troubles, but
I am still alive, healthy, and doing well in life,

And I am happily and boldly.

Walking down the path behind my house
Thoughts filled my head of the bitter past
Images of the past jogging away from my thoughts and shadow

And I am so happy my positive thoughts and resilience brought me to this point in my life.

Cheers to life, and don't give up yet!

There are better days ahead, so smile, pray, and wait.

Nana Adu-Boafo Jnr

Neleke McDermott

We had not long celebrated Mel's 30th birthday. No one would expect the news we were about to receive.

Mel had a lump on her breast that she found when she was 20 years old. She went to 6 different GPs who told her she was too young for it to be cancer and that it was just a cyst, so she left it. When she was 30, she went traveling and met Conar in Thailand. She fell in love and came back to Australia to plan her move to Colorado, USA. While preparing, she decided to go to the doctor to check out the lump. They were concerned and did a biopsy. Four days later, they told her that she had stage 4 breast cancer and needed to have a mastectomy.

It was a Friday, and we met Mel at the park. We met at the park with two friends, Sky and Sally. Mel knew what she wanted to do, and we all worked together to figure out how to get her and her van to Melbourne to be with her mom and family. You need your family when going through something like this. Mel loved Connor and didn't want Connor to feel like he had the pressure of being her support system, especially as he was so far away. So she broke it off with him.

I heard about Vipassana. I remember my client telling me that it makes you more loving, compassionate, understanding, present, and patient. This is what I wanted to be for my friend. So I went for ten days in silence to Vipassana. It was Christmas, and it was so hard for me to come to terms with being present when you are constantly thinking that it may be your best friend's last Christmas.

Mel went through 12 months of chemo and eight weeks of intense radiation, with a 2-week break. We went to Bali for some fun in the sun, and then she came back to 12 months of Herceptin. Mel said it was too much; she was sick of feeling sick for three weeks a month and only well for one week. She refused the final two months. Mel wanted to explore CBD, which was not an option in Australia. It was in Colorado, so she went to the USA for three months, reunited with Connor, and went to Colorado to stay with Connor and his family because CBD was legal. This part of her journey with cancer, I remember being her happiest; she loved Connor.

Mel always said she wanted to spend her last year in the bush, surrounded by peace and nature. After Vipassana, Mel told me that my energy was like a raging bushfire that would engulf everything, but after Vipassana, it was like a campfire that you could sit around and toast marshmallows. I had packed up my house to move to Brisbane for work. I asked Mel, "Do you want to live with me? If you do, I will stay and look after you until the end." Mel said yes, and we unpacked.

Hospice brought a bed, and we put it in the lounge, looking over the swimming pool. I knew my friend was coming to the pointy end of the stick, so I called all my friends and family to come and pour love all over her. Our nearest and dearest came and respectfully said their farewells.

What helped me to stay resilient was balance: work, exercise, family, and friends. I told Mel my heart told me to spend every second with her, but my head said I needed to keep everything else in my life. This would maybe make it easier for me when she leaves. In the beginning, I could work full time and go to the gym every day, but slowly, I worked less and less, went to the gym less, and saw friends and family less.

Ongoing challenges. Managing people's need to spend time with Mel as she deteriorated and managing her as she deteriorated so that she still felt independent and in control. People wanted to come to say their farewells, be close to Mel, and for her to feel the love and support they had for her while she wanted more and more space. Anxiety from others made Mel physically sick, and as her appetite diminished and she got smaller, we were mindful not only of who she would see but also of the number of people she saw. We can all relate to when you're sick, and people ask, "How are you? Can I get anything for you?" you know you need help but still respond with "I'm okay," and you soldier on and look after yourself. So, I came up with a number system: 1 being the worst and five stars being the best. We agreed it's a less charged way to ask, and we would start our day with me saying, "What number, Melsy?" I would do everything if she was a 1, and if she was a 5, she could have her space to take as little or as long to make breakfast, shower, take her medication, and spend time with friends and family.

Personal growth. Mel loved her mom, dad, brother, and family, but she chose me. I wanted my friend to experience what my mom, dad, and family would do for me: make sure I had every comfort I needed, treatments, fun, rest, love, and no worry. I didn't know that I had learned this from my family, but I did know that I had to be strong for Mel every day and put everything into perspective and priorities. We had counselling with a Buddhist counsellor separately and together to keep us present and not cry about all of our wonderful times with each other and cry about what we will miss out on because she won't be around very long.

The last two months went by so fast. I was now only working two days a week. I invited a friend or family of Mel's choice to come and help me for a day or 2. We had an SOP and information, so they were informed, and Mel could feel supported.

I called Connor in the USA; he said Mel didn't tell him how sick she was. I invited him to stay. Connor came with his mom for two weeks. It was so good for Mel; she was happy, slept well, and laughed a lot. It was beautiful to see.

Mel didn't want to celebrate her birthday, but everyone wanted to wish her a happy birthday. How do we make that happen? I thought, wouldn't it be great if all our friends could come and dance and sing and wish Mel happy birthday?

With only five days to organize, I went to Kawana Stadium, and they said I could invite people to come. We went on the radio and, in the paper, dropped flyers all around the Sunshine Coast, inviting everyone. I wanted Mel to see all her friends, family, and the awesome community of people come and do something extraordinary for her birthday. Over 500 people showed up, sang, and danced. We had five camera crews and edited a video and testimonials to show Mel on her birthday. On Monday, we showed her, and it was beautiful how happy it made her and to see her excited to see all of the people that we know and some we hadn't seen for over ten years that came to wish her a happy birthday.

Mel called me at work and asked me to come home. It was the first time that I'd heard her so upset. When I got home, she said that she could feel herself dying and that she was scared. It was one of the most emotional days we had.

The following two weeks, I told myself that for me to be there for Mel, I needed to reschedule all of my emotions for when she left. I didn't suppress them; I just put them on hold. My poor darling was only around 40kgs, having fewer lucid moments.

Hospice brought a bed, and we put it in the lounge, looking over the swimming pool. I knew my friend was coming to the pointy end of the stick, so I called all my friends and family to come and pour love all over her. Our nearest and dearest came and respectfully said their farewells.

I knew now that I needed help and had support, and RNs came. It was their first and last night. It was 7 am; I was talking to Mel. I asked her if she wanted me to sing her a song; she turned her head and looked at me, so I held her hand. She took three deep breaths and then never took another.

Neleke McDermott

Patricia Saville

This is the day that broke my family, and nothing has been the same since. The day my little brother, Dakota, passed away.

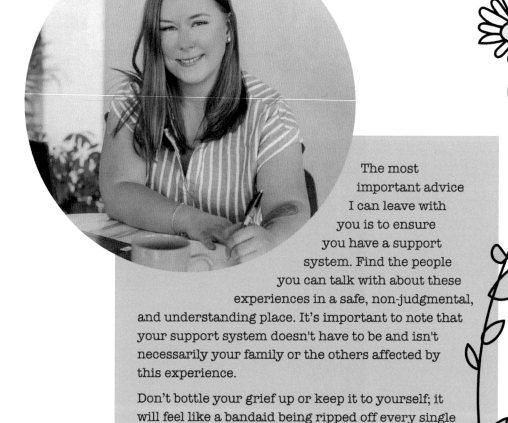

The most important advice I can leave with you is to ensure you have a support system. Find the people you can talk with about these experiences in a safe, non-judgmental, and understanding place. It's important to note that your support system doesn't have to be and isn't necessarily your family or the others affected by this experience.

Don't bottle your grief up or keep it to yourself; it will feel like a bandaid being ripped off every single time. Take it at your own pace, day by day, moment by moment.

I remember it as if it was yesterday.

It was 10:30 pm, and I was dropping my dad's car off at his place. The main intersection down the road from the house I grew up in was blocked off. There was a lot of traffic and emergency cars, so I decided to take a shortcut and go around.

Once I dropped off the car, I started walking back to my place and walked through the main intersection I had avoided. While waiting to cross the street, I instantly felt that something bad had happened there. I looked over to the cleared accident area and noticed a skateboard on the ground. My little brother used a longboard to get around town. At that moment at the intersection, I swore it looked like a skateboard and felt relieved. I found out later that I was wrong; it was a longboard.

This was the first point in the night I had *hope*.

When I got home, I jumped in the shower. Once I got out, I saw I had a voicemail from my mom.

My gut dropped.

I listened to it and heard her say in a calm voice, *'Dakota has been hurt. Call me back.'* Instantly, I knew the accident at the intersection was him, and my head started spinning.

I called her back, but she didn't say much except to contact my dad and get us to meet her at my little sister's hotel. I called my dad at least ten times, if not more, and his girlfriend as well until he finally picked up. I told him about the call with my mom and told him to come get me.

My dad had to drive through the intersection to pick me up. As he was pulling up, he just kept yelling and crying and saying that Dakota was dead. I repeatedly told him no, Dakota would be fine, and that he was just hurt.

I had *hope*.

We got to the hotel, and while my parents were talking to the cops, my sister Rikki got into the car with me. After what felt like forever, our dad returned and said we were going to the hospital. At this time, I was working at the hospital as a housekeeper. I actually had just gotten Dakota a job there as a porter. We drove in silence, and then he turned in the opposite direction of the hospital. I asked him where we were going, and he said New Westminster.

My heart dropped.

The hospital in Abbotsford was a fairly new building at this time and had top-of-the-line equipment, so I knew this wasn't a good sign that we were going to New Westminster.

However, I continued to have *hope*.

When we finally got to the hospital, it was like an out-of-body experience. I had tunnel vision as a cop walked us through the halls. The hospital was busy and noisy, yet there was a deafening silence. I briefly saw a couple of our aunts in a small room on the way. They hugged us quickly, and I noticed a couple of Dakota's friends were there too. I later found out that his friends were at the scene, but I didn't see them when I walked past as they were behind a bush talking to the cops.

To this day, walking into that room, I experienced the worst sound of my life that still rings in my ear today — hearing my mother crying for her child.

It's a sound that shoots right up your back, causes the hair on your arms to go up, you're paralyzed with pain, you can't catch your breath, and it's like you've been stabbed straight through your heart.

I saw my mom draped by Dakota's body as he lay lifeless on the stretcher hooked up to machines. My dad howled in pain at the scene. My little sister and I stood in shock. I saw all my older siblings standing silently. Some were crying, and others were stoic. I won't go further into the details of Dakota's physical state, but the image is burned in my mind and still haunts me to this day.

But still, I had *hope*.

I thought, *'He just needs to rest, to heal his body. The doctors will figure out the best way to help him. It will be a long battle, but he will get better.'*

We went to the small room where my aunts and Dakota's friends were, and we waited together for the doctor to update us. When the doctor finally came, he gave us the news...

Dakota died at the scene and was brain-dead. He wasn't coming back. They were just keeping him alive for us to say goodbye and so he could donate his organs. As they weren't able to keep his blood pressure up, he was only able to donate his eyes.

My world shattered. My *hope* was gone.

After that, everything was a blur. We each got the chance to say our goodbyes. I can clearly remember when they turned off the machines. I felt the warmth leave Dakota's left hand that I held until it went cold. I looked up at the clock — 2:15 am.

I was the last one in the room. I don't know how long I was there after he was gone and everyone had left. I stood up and started to walk out, but then turned around and took a few steps back toward him. I did this a few times as I didn't want to leave him alone. It was so hard leaving the room where my baby brother's body lay.

My little brother, Dakota Leslie, died on May 1st, 2015 at 19 years old.

This is the day that broke my family, and nothing has been the same since.

It took over three years to come out of a state of sleepwalking, where I was stuck on autopilot. Multiple deaths happened around Dakota's death, which played a role in why it took so long for me to heal. Plus, I moved to Vancouver shortly after on my own. That's a story for another time.

It took eight years to truly feel 'normal' again. To have *hope* again.

They say time heals. I loathe this saying. Time is a construct we've created for ourselves in society to move through life. This saying is a comforting statement people say to help you feel better. Because with time, people forget. Not you or the people immediately affected, but everyone else. It's a harsh reality of life.

Over time, do you heal? Yes, but only if you put the work in.

Do you get back to normal? No, you never go back, only forward. You grow and learn to live with it.

You create a new normal.

My journey of healing from Dakota's death has been the most difficult chapter of my life. The most challenging adjustment has been when you hear a song play or smell something familiar that brings up a memory — the grief, the gut-wrenching pain, and the guilt of forgetting your loved one is gone. These feelings come back immensely despite how happy you may have been feeling. As that moment passes, you will realize that this is a part of the process; *you are healing*.

Just remember to always let yourself feel these moments. Remind yourself that it is okay. And you continue to live and allow yourself to be happy because we are resilient, and there is *hope*.

It took a while to practice resilience, and I give myself grace because resilience isn't linear; it's individual. We all have unique experiences and process them differently. I'm consciously and constantly working on healing myself, letting myself feel, helping others on their journey, and continuing to talk about Dakota to others to keep his memory alive as much as possible while still living my own life.

The most important advice I can leave with you is to ensure you have a support system. Find the people you can talk with about these experiences in a safe, non-judgmental, and understanding place. It's important to note that your support system doesn't have to be and isn't necessarily your family or the others affected by this experience. Don't bottle your grief up or keep it to yourself; it will feel like a bandaid being ripped off every single time. Take it at your own pace, day by day, moment by moment.

There is no timeline for healing.

Patricia Saville

Pri Lewis

When it's your own story, reflecting on resiliency can be tricky as it is easier to see it in others than yourself. Overcoming and embracing challenges or doing things that may be a little crazy is innately who I have always been.

> Life sometimes requires you to dig deep and tap into your resiliency toolkit. My life had prepared me to approach this time with a determined mindset and an unwavering commitment to finding solutions.

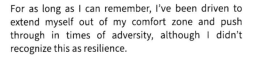

For as long as I can remember, I've been driven to extend myself out of my comfort zone and push through in times of adversity, although I didn't recognize this as resilience.

When I was 16, my parents decided to move to the US. I chose to stay in the UK alone and attend college. It should have been daunting, but it was one of those things I just did. My mothers' words to me as I made this life-changing decision echoed in my mind, "You screw it up, and it's on you." These words, although stern, became a driving force, compelling me to strive for success.

I lived in shared housing, worked full-time in the evenings, went to college every day, and partied most nights. I was burning the candle at both ends but living my best life. I took challenges in my stride and never questioned whether things would work out; I just made them happen, but some may see it as being resilient. I passed my driving test, completed college, and went on to get a BSc in Psychology, and I didn't screw it up.

The few years, summed up in a paragraph, goes something like this...

2002: I met my husband at university.

2005: Left a perfectly amazing career working with at-risk youth and moved to Greece with Lewi when he bought a bar with his best friend.

2005: On a whim and pushing those comfort zones, I started a photography company in Greece, knowing very little about the subject other than taking holiday pics, never questioning if it would work. This company became successful and supported me for the next four years.

2005-2008: Lewi and I spent our time between Greece and Whistler. We were skiing the coastal mountains in the winter and running our business in Greece in the summer.

In 2008, browsing the local newspaper in Whistler, I came across a 1-line advertisement, "restaurant space for lease." It caught my eye, and I immediately called the number. Within a few hours, we had viewed the restaurant space, secured a 3rd partner, our good friend Alex, and prepared an offer to lease. We threw in our savings, and with 20k, we opened our first restaurant, Three Below.

With a lot of heart, hard work, and hustle, Three Below became a well-loved local establishment in Whistler. In 2014, we opened our second restaurant, The Brickworks, and in 2017, Main Street Noodles. During this time, I married the love of my life and had two kiddos!

Being an entrepreneur has always come with its fair share of obstacles, but my ultimate test of resiliency came to a head in 2020. COVID-19 challenged the world but became a pivotal turning point in my life. As a business owner, I faced an unimaginable reality— our businesses were mandated to close their doors. The uncertainty loomed large: When would we reopen? How would we pay the bills? Were we on the brink of losing everything?

Sometimes, our resilience can push us to our limits, leading to a breakdown before a breakthrough, and this is exactly what happened to me. I had never experienced anxiety until 2020. I felt so hopeless and out of control. Our lives and everything we had built were at risk and in the hands of others; this was an unfamiliar feeling that I did not like. My mindset remained determined, but the obstacles were relentless. I was consumed with ensuring we followed the rules, came up with ideas to do more, sell more, and pivot where we could. I was on high alert and in survival mode 24-7, barrelling through without much regard for my own well-being. In May of 2020, we held a companywide meeting at Brickworks. I was overwhelmed, and the weight of the world felt like it was on my shoulders. As I walked in and saw the faces of the people who were looking to me for answers, I felt a rush of an unknown feeling. I turned and walked out and experienced my first-ever panic attack. It was an out-of-body experience, like electricity was travelling through me, and I had no control. At that moment, my body and mind were telling me that the way I was living was not sustainable and that something needed to change.

The anxiety that surfaced in 2020 has become a constant companion, rewiring my body and needing daily love and attention. While devastating to my objectives at the time, the shutting down of the restaurants served as the catalyst for my path of self-discovery and a redefined perception of life. I've gone from an inherently successful but unbalanced life to one driven by intentional action, all while consciously working to shape my future.

Life sometimes requires you to dig deep and tap into your resiliency toolkit. My life had prepared me to approach this time with a determined mindset and an unwavering commitment to finding solutions.

My advice to those navigating similar challenges is to understand that resilience is deeper than overcoming obstacles. The notion of facing and overcoming adversity teaches you lessons that lead to impactful growth that can transform you and your perspective on life.

Pri Lewis

Sam van Born

During unprecedented challenges over the last three years as a first responder, I faced PTSD. This journey intersected my passion for natural health products and helped me advocate for wellness and recovery. It was my personal mission to heal.

WELCOME TO THE *family*

To practice resilience, I connect, whether it's with friends, family, or my daughter, or I see how I can work on my business to help others!! I go out and walk daily, rain or shine..or snow!! I focus on putting great nutrition into my body, getting enough water, and getting a good night's sleep. Routine is extremely helpful. I continue to lean into the essence of my business, wellness and also respecting my mind & body's limits and needs during recovery.

Being a frontline worker in the fire service during the pandemic, my mental health was tested to the max, and I realized it was time for me to take a knee and focus on myself.

I was drowning.

Twenty-four years of being in a brother and sisterhood of "I've got your back" and the feeling of you'll always be taken care of was broken. It was during the height of the pandemic. It was when I, and everyone in the world, were tested to their max. We were unsure of what we were dealing with, and the fear was starting to build: what was right, what wasn't? What was the best way to keep ourselves safe? Everything was heightened; every little thing was under a microscope, creating challenges within our culture.

The calls got longer and more frequent, and we could not help in ways that seemed simpler before. It was starting to fracture. The calls that may not have been so bothersome started to stick. And it wasn't until that very support system personally challenged me and I had to take a knee. I had hit my max. I couldn't drive by certain locations, constantly thinking about the outcomes of certain calls, people who had passed, how it would affect their families, kids, etc.

Why, how, nothing was making a difference. The whole world was sad, and I couldn't trust anyone anymore and felt completely alone.

I walked away, nine months to be exact. And it took me some time to start feeling like myself again. I reached out for support, and even that took time to fall into place. Every step took so much time and patience that I truly could relate to why some give up.

The diagnosis of PTSD was ultimately the outcome, and I found a great counselor to help me navigate what I was feeling and experiencing. Multiple traumas can be quite a muddy mess to wade through. But it was time for me to put myself first for myself and my daughter.

I had meetings twice a week and sometimes took my day minute by minute. I started walking; I needed that connection with other people. I needed the validation that I wasn't alone. Seeing people at their worst and only being able to help for a short while, not knowing the outcome of most calls, nothing ever seemed final in the sense of us as not knowing the outcome of most calls. How were the people doing that we helped?

So, I started focusing on my business. It was another way for me to continue to help people, another way for me to make a difference. Naturopathically formulated health products, yes!! Seeing a change in people's health, reducing inflammation, improving gut health, weight management, and good clean energy. It was making a difference. With good nutrition in my body, I started to feel better. When I was out walking and making eye contact with others, seeing them acknowledge and smile back were the simple things that started adding back to my cup.

Being able to give back and help others, in turn, was also helping me heal. I have been back to work now for almost two years. I am closer to retirement now, and I am excited to see where my business will continue to grow.

How can I continue to help others get into a better place? I will continue to help & support others because I know if you don't take care of your health (both physical & mental), you have nothing. Starting by putting great nutrition into your body will help shift you into a better mindset. Health maintenance vs digging yourself out of a health crisis is the way things are shifting. I'd love to help you get to a good place; let's talk. Don't get to a place where you feel alone and too overwhelmed. I'm here to help.

"The best investment you'll ever make is in your own health."

I think people also need to understand that PTSD doesn't just affect first responders; everyday people can also be affected by trauma. It doesn't have to be a big traumatic event. Anyone can experience trauma. It's a distressing event and the inability to cope. It affects everyone in different ways.

To practice resilience, I connect, whether it's with friends, family, or my daughter, or I see how I can work on my business to help others!! I go out and walk daily, rain or shine..or snow!! I focus on putting great nutrition into my body, getting enough water, and getting a good night's sleep. Routine is extremely helpful. I continue to lean into the essence of my business, wellness and also respecting my mind & body's limits and needs during recovery.

You are not alone. Advocate fiercely for your own healing. Embrace being vulnerable and foster connections; you will be surprised how empowering and healing it is to share your story.

| Sam van Born

Saskia Christian

Amidst the haunting void left by my dad's disappearance, I navigated the labyrinth of life, defying the weight of his parental absence, as I forged ahead in the pursuit of a future defined by my defiant strength and unshakeable resilience.

The Vanishing

Encircled by the serenity of a tranquil lake in my neighborhood forest, my heart was beset with worry. I had received distressing news earlier that day – my father, who had been battling with mental issues for years, was missing. Thoughts raced through my mind, and I couldn't shake that feeling of helplessness.

That daunting feeling of my dad never coming home swept over me. How could he have vanished without a trace? Why didn't anyone see him where he occasionally hung out on the bustling streets of Georgetown? I became more disillusioned as time went on. Could this be my dad's demise?

His absence transformed me, with resilience, authenticity, and fulfillment as my guiding forces. Embracing my true self, I pursued my passions and found fulfillment. The support from loved ones and the healing power of nature brought solace. Through my pain, I discovered a purpose - advocating for trauma victims and becoming a beacon of hope.

I was sickened to the pit of my stomach. My vivid recollection of my father's distraught state during our last call was very unsettling. Did he lose his memory because of his mental agony?

In the face of his heart-wrenching disappearance, I found myself thrust into a world where resilience became my steadfast companion, guiding me through the darkest nights and empowering me to embrace the flickering light of hope as I navigated the labyrinth of life with defiant strength and an unyielding spirit. Thankfully, I also found solace in the untouched wilderness around me.

As I ventured deeper into the forest, I stumbled upon a hidden clearing. In the heart of the clearing, I found myself drawn towards a small, weathered bench. I sat down, my heart racing with anticipation. Closing my eyes, I focused on my father's deep voice and summoned memories of his laughter. And at that moment, amidst the stillness of the forest, I thought I heard it – a faint whisper carried on the wind as if my father's deep voice was calling out to me. "Hey, Saskie!"

Tears streamed down my face as I felt a mix of relief and sorrow. I knew my journey wasn't over and that finding my father would need strength, resilience, and the support of others. But sitting in that sacred space, I felt a glimmer of hope and made a silent promise to myself not to give up on finding him.

For decades, I had refused to accept the extent of my dad's mental issues due to fear of stigmatization until that Sunday when I had to face the reality. He had called me frantically that day, complaining about his neighbors trying to steal his identity. I struggled to make sense of it all. I pleaded with him to tell me what help he needed to overcome his struggles. Imagine not being able to resolve your parent's pain. Even though that feeling of helplessness was painful, I can't conceptualize the distress my father was enduring.

A Desperate Quest

That Sunday phone call was the last time I spoke with my dad years ago. I kept his voicemail, which led to our call for years until it became unbearable. That call ushered in a long, desperate quest for answers about my dad's location. I reached out to his family and friends. No one knew exactly his whereabouts.

My desperation intensified, pushing me to seek the help of private investigators. I clung to the belief that these professionals would uncover the truth and bring my father back alive. I felt somehow that despite having several ailments, my father would make it through. After all, he had always bounced back with amazing managerial opportunities. Why wouldn't he be alive?

The Elusive Answers

Despite the private investigators' best efforts, the trail leading to my father vanished into thin air. Every lead I followed led to dead ends, and frustration clawed at my resolve. Eventually, I accepted that my father would never be discovered. The weight of unanswered questions threatened to consume me, but I knew I had to find a way to continue living my life and fulfill my destiny.

A New Direction

As I grappled with my father's absence, I found solace in my chemical engineering career. The intricacies of my work became a refuge. Despite the void looming in my heart, my determination to succeed in life grew stronger. I needed to be the one to accomplish what my dad couldn't, even though he had immense talent.

But deep within me, a new calling began to emerge. I realized that my journey of resilience and strength could inspire others facing similar hardships. I made the courageous decision to transition from my successful engineering career to become a Trauma and Resilience Life Coach, using my experiences to empower and uplift those who yearned for guidance. My empathy and understanding enabled me to guide others toward embracing their strength, even in the face of unanswered questions.

Embracing the Unanswered

On my journey, my father's disappearance haunted me. Years passed, and the answers remained elusive. Amidst the pain, I found solace in the unanswered questions. Closure eluded me, but I made peace with this reality.

His absence transformed me, with resilience, authenticity, and fulfillment as my guiding forces. Embracing my true self, I pursued my passions and found fulfillment. The support from loved ones and the healing power of nature brought solace. Through my pain, I discovered a purpose - advocating for trauma victims and becoming a beacon of hope.

My story is a testament to the unwavering strength of the human spirit, a reminder of our resilience. Let the echoes of "Resilient Authentic Fulfillment" reverberate within us, reminding us of the shared understanding and boundless possibilities on life's extraordinary journey.

Saskia Christian

Shannon Mitchell

COVID-19 shut down the world just as I moved to Kamloops, a brand-new city.

My advice to any of those people reading this and pondering – hmmmm, is drinking affecting my life? Take a look at truly what is happening in YOUR life and go for the sober life: clarity, better connections with those you love, and the internal resilience of STRENGTH.

My journey toward sobriety wasn't just about giving up alcohol; it was my courageous decision that transformed my entire world. Almost four years ago (celebrating January 1, 2024), I made a life-altering choice to quit drinking. My determination stemmed from a deep desire to provide my twins, Lauren and Davis, a better life, secure my career, and ultimately reclaim control over my life.

Before I decided to quit drinking, my life was in a haze of alcohol-induced chaos. My dependence on the socially acceptable red wine had begun to dictate my actions and decisions. Every day was a struggle, a battle between my addiction and my responsibilities. But my turning point arrived when I realized the toll drinking was taking on Lauren and Davis. What kind of role model was I being?

Lauren and Davis are my world, and their innocent eyes mirrored the pain and confusion caused by my choices. It was a wake-up call I couldn't ignore. I knew I needed to break free from the shackles of alcohol to be the supportive, loving, EPIC mom they deserved.

It was so interesting – I went to doctors and counselors, and they all said, "Oh, you don't have a problem – your marriage just fell apart, you are a single mom raising twins – go have fun. Just don't drink alone, set some boundaries around alcohol. I got a pass to drink wine from the most trusted professionals!

I found an app online and made pledges daily to stay sober, and at the end of each day, the app did a check-in. Very helpful! And a great reminder of MY WHY!!

Almost four years into sobriety, my life has been transformational. Davis and Lauren now see a mother who is present, engaged, and filled with an abundance of love. I decided to change careers, move to another city, and start a new life for all of us. I have a newfound confidence and a sense of inner peace, and people are now choosing for their lives to give NO DRINKING a go! I love this for them – Stephens and Marcie – you have been gifts in my life, and I am so thankful for your friendships.

My journey has taught me valuable lessons—about resilience, about the power of love, and about tapping into the inner strength within oneself.

My advice to any of those people reading this and pondering – hmmmm, is drinking affecting my life? Take a look at truly what is happening in YOUR life and go for the sober life: clarity, better connections with those you love, and the internal resilience of STRENGTH.

Shannon Mitchell

Shannon Villalba

I had been suffering for six months without any answers, and here was the answer I was expecting, "You have cancer."

The moment I saw my oncologist's face as she walked in the door and looked at me, my life changed. In my heart, I knew it was true, but I didn't want to believe it. Three words resounded in my head as I cried on my mother's shoulder, her multicolored sweater softening with my tears. I have cancer. Images of my son growing up, places I loved, and family floated in my head. I felt numb, as if in a dream, and my doctor's words were a blur. I wasn't ready to leave this world. As I sat there crying, I felt a spark in my heart. The warrior in me called out, "We will fight. We will fight with everything we have; even when we're down, we won't ever give up."

It was a few days before Christmas and my son's birthday, so I was determined to hide my feelings as much as I could so my son could enjoy his holiday. We went and saw Star Wars, but I was numb. The shock of it all kept me in a daze. As I watched the ships battle it out on the screen, warrior me repeated, "We fight. We fight for moments like these." Through the shock and numbness, I was angry. Thoughts raced through my head: I am young, why me, why now? Haven't I gone through enough as a single parent to a medically handicapped child? Haven't I fought enough for myself after being treated poorly and devalued by others?" Even worse, after my initial diagnosis, my doctor kept stating that more tests needed to be done because my cells looked different.

Sure enough, it was worse, way worse. It was small-cell cervical cancer at an advanced stage and growing fast. This made me even more angry. I was angry, sad, and afraid all at the same time. I screamed at the world like a toddler in a tantrum, beating my hands against the wall; dropping to my knees, I wailed incoherently as rivers of tears flowed down my face. Other times, I closeted myself away, my entire body shaking irrepressibly with fear. But after calming down, with resolve, I knew I had to do everything in my power to stay alive, to be with my son and my family, and to experience life.

I was scrappy and independent, but I knew I could not fight alone this time. After telling my family and close friends, I made a declaration on my Facebook page about my diagnosis and that I would fight and be clear in five months. With all my heart, I believed I would endure and embrace all the help I received. I initially did not want to do chemotherapy and wanted to focus solely on using holistic treatments because of the serious side effects. My diagnosis left me feeling out of control, and I desired to assume responsibility for my treatment and experience. However, upon learning from fellow survivors about the fatalities of those solely relying on holistic approaches, combined with persistent family pressure to undergo chemotherapy, I reassessed my decision. Thus, I put together a strategy I could follow with my doctor's recommendations. I adamantly stated, "If you want me to put this poison in my body, then I'm going to do everything else on my terms."

Unwaveringly, I would do everything in my power to have some semblance of control. Consequently, I opened my mind to various ways I could heal physically, mentally, and spiritually since I wanted to attack the cancer on every level. I changed my diet and practiced various types of meditation techniques, crystal healing, sound healing, and mindfulness.

Throughout my journey to practice resilience, I used many holistic therapies to put my mind in a healing state, kept an open mind, and allowed others to participate in assisting me. I meditated daily using affirmations and prayers and envisioned multiple ways to heal my body. Meditation helped my mind shift from fighting the cancer to loving the cancer. Once I made that shift, the cancer left.

Every time I entered the infusion center I came armed with essential oils, fuzzy socks, a warm blanket, crystals, and a speaker to play healing music. Friends and family joined me. I set the stage for healing within the room to benefit me and the other women. I envisioned every type of fictional and historical character fighting that cancer as the chemo pulsed through me.

My sister set up a calendar, and friends would come and cook for me and my son, help clean, and take care of me. Friends and family put me on prayer lists. When I did my daily meditations, I tapped into the collective energy of healing and love, feeling it undulate and pulse through me, diminishing cancer on a spiritual level. This comforting love enveloped me and gave me hope on some of my darkest days.

My doctor gave me surprising news after the first round of chemo and surgery. The combination of holistic therapies with traditional medicine reduced my cancer by 50%! I still had a long road ahead, especially with keeping my mind focused on healing and not on dying. It was a constant emotional rollercoaster to temper my thoughts towards focusing on the healing aspect. At one point between the radiation and chemotherapy, I felt myself dying, slipping between the veils. I felt the looming spectre of death in my room, getting closer to me every day.

I thought, "If cancer doesn't kill me, these "treatments" will." Determinedly, I pushed back on my doctors to give me a break, which is what I needed. This also gave me time to focus on my holistic therapies and develop specific healing strategies that assisted and eased my mental state.

Due to my extensive experience in meditation, I crafted meditations that ranged from imagining myself dancing through fire to burn cancer to waves of colors wafting through my body, raising my vibration with every color change. These meditations, coupled with the love from my son, dog, family, and friends, allowed me to alter my perspective and envelop myself in the collective healing effort. At this time, I switched from fighting the cancer to loving it. I embraced it with my entire being and thanked it for the lessons it was giving me.

During my final chemo session, I hugged myself and caressed my abdomen, stating, "Thank you; it's time for you to leave." My mind was at peace, and I felt a dramatic shift not only in my body but in the vibration of my being. My final scan occurred five months after my public declaration that I would be healed. The words I spoke were true - I was cancer-free!

Throughout my journey to practice resilience, I used many holistic therapies to put my mind in a healing state, kept an open mind, and allowed others to participate in assisting me. I meditated daily using affirmations and prayers and envisioned multiple ways to heal my body. Meditation helped my mind shift from fighting the cancer to loving the cancer. Once I made that shift, the cancer left.

My advice to you is to love yourself and give yourself grace for things out of your control. By loving yourself more, you can forgive yourself and others, bringing yourself peace. Inner peace gives you the clarity to formulate a strategy that works for you and grants you the strength and resolve you need.

Shannon Villalba

Shelly Lynn Hughes

My marriage dissolved, I became a single parent, and my health suffered.

Five years ago marked a pivotal juncture in my life, a period defined by profound challenges that ultimately became the catalyst for a transformative journey of resilience and self-discovery. The dissolution of my marriage, coupled with the responsibilities of being a full-time parent to two young daughters—one of whom has autism and severe food allergies— plunged me into the uncharted territory of solitude.

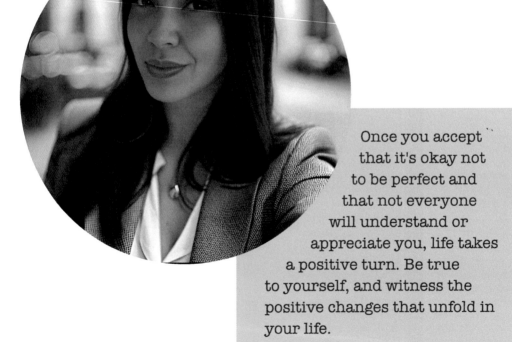

Once you accept that it's okay not to be perfect and that not everyone will understand or appreciate you, life takes a positive turn. Be true to yourself, and witness the positive changes that unfold in your life.

Simultaneously, my physical health took a backseat, my business encountered setbacks, and the daunting task of relocating homes loomed large. To compound the difficulties, my father was battling stage 4 cancer. It was an exceptionally trying and isolating chapter that unprecedentedly pushed the boundaries of my resilience.

Amid this tumult, tears were a rare occurrence. Having weathered numerous tribulations, I had become desensitized to my own emotions. Yet, around three months into this challenging period, I consciously decided to draw strength from within. I resolved not to succumb to the adversities before me, understanding the critical importance of persevering—not only for the sake of my daughters but, perhaps more crucially, for my well-being.

Fast forward five years, and the transformation is nothing short of remarkable. Two bestselling books, the creation of an extraordinary community spanning five countries, the acquisition of a car through my efforts, a 40-pound weight loss, and the restoration of my health stand as tangible evidence of the resilience I summoned during that challenging time. I now find myself in a state of unparalleled happiness.

The journey was undoubtedly arduous yet immensely rewarding. My life is far from perfect today, but it is a testament to the power of resilience and our choices in the face of adversity. Reflecting on my experiences, I am acutely aware that many others are navigating their own challenging paths. To those currently facing difficulties, I offer a reminder that even when it seems you've reached your limit, there exists an opportunity to rise above and make a choice—every single day.

My life, while not flawless, is undeniably fulfilling. It is, in fact, the best it has ever been. The journey demanded hard work and unwavering determination, and I am a living testament to the transformative power of resilience. Regardless of your current struggles, understand that you possess the capacity to shape your narrative and carve a path toward a brighter future.

Embrace authenticity without fear. My most significant successes and personal growth occurred when I acknowledged my flaws while recognizing the awesomeness within. Once you accept that it's okay not to be perfect and that not everyone will understand or appreciate you, life takes a positive turn. Be true to yourself, and witness the positive changes that unfold in your life.

Once you accept that it's okay not to be perfect and that not everyone will understand or appreciate you, life takes a positive turn. Be true to yourself, and witness the positive changes that unfold in your life.

| Shelly Lynn Hughes

Shmiko Cole

From a young age, I knew I didn't fit into any "box." I believe that it helped to shape my life mission from an early age.

I am Shmiko, a living mosaic of cultures. Born into a world where my existence is a blend of distinct heritages, I am a living embodiment of how belief systems can come together for a common purpose. It is now my daily mission to be an equitable gatekeeper and use the resilience I learned, breaking through many proverbial glass ceilings to open doors for the new rising stars of today.

My journey of self-discovery led me to a profound realization: embracing both sides of my identity is not just an act of balance but a celebration of my unique path. I honor my position as a bridge between many worlds.

My life has been a dance of colors and customs, filled with the intersections of divergent cultures. But this dance has not been without its missteps and stumbles. Code-switching and understanding how to adapt to different situations were critical to finding success on my journey. Words and gestures, so clear in one culture, could become distorted or misinterpreted through the lens of another. I faced stereotypes that tried to confine me within narrow boundaries based on my appearance and the cultural tags I carried. I was often challenged by the weight of expectations, torn between conforming to cultural norms and staying true to my values. I consistently chose the latter and planned my path accordingly. I remember the perplexed looks when I switched languages mid-sentence or merged traditions in unexpected ways. I learned very young to be an effective code mixer, which prepared me well for the challenges I would face in my career.

I entered retail management and the corporate world at a young age. In the 1990s, as a multicultural woman, I was shut out of many opportunities. Daily, I encountered biases, subtle yet persistent, which shaped my connections and career development. Colleagues were unwilling to train or support me, and I had to work twice as hard (or more) to prove my worthiness, time and again.

"Harmony in Hues" traces my story. I saw firsthand how hard it was for women of color, especially the few of us with multicultural backgrounds, to be heard and to be given opportunities for advancement. I often felt pressured to adopt a singular cultural identity, to blend in rather than stand out. I knew that I had to keep fighting to be listened to and taken seriously in the white and male-dominated work culture. I had to break the glass ceilings, clean up the shards, and open the doors and windows for others like me who weren't being invited to the proverbial tables.

Yet, in every challenge, I found a hidden opportunity. I refused to let others' expectations and narrow perceptions of me and those who looked like me hold me and others back. If anything, it made me stronger as I learned to navigate these cultural mazes with resilience and openness. Every misunderstanding became a chance for dialogue, every stereotype a moment to educate, and every expectation I exceeded developed even deeper feelings of stewardship within me. I became committed to paving a smoother path behind me for others to follow.

I challenged societal norms, choosing to live as a testament to the value and added perspectives that diversity brings. Once I began to be heard, I was able to create tangible impacts in the workplace. Yet I still knew I wanted more autonomy and control to create opportunities and support for others I never had. Now, as a female multicultural business owner of a global company, I intentionally clear the trail for diverse talent to bloom with their skill sets. I consider myself one of the new legacy gatekeepers and take the position seriously.

Some folks now call what I do in the business world "magic," but it wasn't purely alchemy. My current success, for myself and others, came at the cost of learning how to use my voice and break down prejudiced barriers while maintaining a balanced home life, my physical health, and raising two sons.

Now, as a CEO and business owner, I can extend the table and add as many chairs as possible. Helping people helps feed my soul and aligns with the sense of purpose I always had as a multicultural person. I went from being gate-kept outside the proverbial palace doors to being a gatekeeper who throws wide the entrances for others and provides support so their skills can be utilized best. Previously, my voice was muffled, but now I can give a voice to the voiceless and provide opportunities to those who previously had few choices.

My journey of self-discovery led me to a profound realization: embracing both sides of my identity is not just an act of balance but a celebration of my unique path. I honor my position as a bridge between many worlds.

My story is one that I hope resonates with anyone who has ever felt caught between cultures, challenged to find their place in a world with prescribed societal "boxes" for people. My journey illustrates the strength that comes from embracing one's uniqueness and the resilience it takes to carve paths where no one "like me" has gone before. I am continuously inspired to lead others to success while proudly celebrating their diverse backgrounds. I move forward with the wisdom of what it took to get here... and how much further we have on this journey towards family legacy.

Shmiko Cole

Stacey Stevens

Fifteen years old, with every creature comfort a girl could want – purple shag carpet, a queen-sized bed, my own TV & a sunset mural on my wall, not to mention the pool in our backyard, nestled behind our modern A-frame house, in a great upper middle-class neighbourhood & a boyfriend my parents didn't like, I left home.

If you're reading this, my advice would be don't be controlled by the limiting beliefs you developed fighting to survive. Use resilience to find who you truly are.

Stubborn, blind, or a bit of both, who knows?

I took three things with me the day I left: A garbage bag of clothes, my father's last words to me predicting a very bleak future, and my response: "Screw you. I'm gonna be a lawyer."

In the short time it took me to walk away from my family home, I knew I needed a tough-as-nails exterior. I walked with my chin high and shoulders back. All the while, I was a scared little girl who was going to learn the skills to survive.

I learned how to live small and hide in plain sight. If they don't see me, they won't bother me.

I understood the importance of being agreeable, not confrontational, especially in an environment filled with anger, drugs, and violence.

I became resourceful. I found places to live, went to school, and worked. I learned who could protect me and who couldn't. I became a chameleon. I was whoever I needed to be in any situation.

I spent a lot of time living inside my head, reflecting on who I had become.

Five years went by before I literally escaped with my life.

As I walked back down that same street - this time toward my family home with my tough-as-nails exterior and a huge chip on my shoulder, I was still that scared little girl, hoping for a happy family reunion, picking up somewhere before where we'd left off.

But everything had changed. Everyone had grown up and moved on.

So, I gathered my wits and took stock of my resources. I started working at a law firm & went to night school to be a paralegal, but THIS time, I wasn't going to play it small. I didn't just want to survive. I had something to prove.

Armed with my defiant promise to my father, this 15-year-old runaway with a high school diploma, two teenage boys, an unemployed husband, two dogs, and not enough money was accepted to law school at 37. I was told I would never be given a law license just before I graduated.

My resiliency kicked in, and I fought. I relied on my survival skills, and again, I succeeded.

I became a lawyer at 40 and thought I could finally take off my resilient armor and be myself. I was wrong. I didn't know who I was. I was always pretending to be strong, detached, and unbreakable. I couldn't turn that off. Life was good, but I wasn't.

Inside, the real me was screaming to get out. I couldn't trust myself enough to let go of my armor and show the world who I really was until now. Resiliency changes you, and you're not the same person when you come through it. You are scared and refuse to put down your armor, so you stay trapped by past limiting beliefs & behaviors until you finally decide to use your resiliency one more time to discover who you truly are.

I faced every challenge with the unwavering belief that I would find a way through. My mindset focused on my ability to persevere, grow, and thrive no matter what I encountered. I survived. My journey to discover who I am is on IG @stacey_lynnes

If you're reading this, my advice would be don't be controlled by the limiting beliefs you developed fighting to survive. Use resilience to find who you truly are.

| Stacey Stevens

Tracy Matthews

Life is too short to put your dreams on hold.

If you align your creative gifts with your passion, anything is possible.

You're not too old or too young. You can find the resources. Don't put your dreams on hold because tomorrow may not come.

When I got the call, I was in shock. I had just seen her thirty minutes before. My friend, Rich, picked up the phone and listened. His Latino skin turned grey, and he said: "Here's her daughter."

I was only 21 and in party mode with my friends, heading down to San Diego for a University formal. I was so confused.

The words made no sense *at all*: "Your mother didn't make it!"

What?? I had JUST seen her thirty minutes before, and she seemed "fine," and I'd just left the hospital. How did she die?

Her legs and feet were so swollen, and she played it off like it was nothing. Did I miss something? She did say she was having trouble breathing – even though she played it off with a big laugh.

How was I to know she had a pulmonary embolism – a blot clot – forming in her once skinny legs?

She was only 45 years old and so full of life. And so full of criticism for her beautiful body that she thought was flawed. The crazy part was that she wasn't sick – just caught up in body dysmorphia.

My heart dropped. I'm gonna puke. My chest hurts so bad.

I picked up the phone and called my brother, then my sister, then asked them to call our three other siblings.

As we rushed to the hospital, disbelief flooded me. *My mom died?*

My mother died of complications and a blood clot after elective surgery: liposuction, a tummy tuck, and reconstructive bladder surgery. I believe the true cause of her death was that she didn't love herself or see how beautiful she was on the inside and outside.

After years of searching for love and a purpose outside of her children, my mother had a lot going for her – a fiancé she loved, a new business venture, six great kids, and something she could call her own.

And right before she was about to have it all, she died.

Losing a mother at a young age is strange. You face mortality and realize that life is too short. I'm 52 years old and remember my mother's vibrant energy as I write this. She was one of the most unlikely people you'd expect to die at a young age. One day, she was here – being the life of the party – and the next day, she was gone.

The biggest lesson that I've learned from the death of my mother is that life is too short to put your dreams on hold. Right after my mother died, I put my life into action. I realized I was setting my dreams on the back burner, so I figured out how to finish school.

My grief was overwhelming, but I knew I could do hard things – working full-time and taking more than a "full load" of classes wasn't easy. My story of resilience starts here because I wanted to prove to myself (and my mother) that I would make my life meaningful. That's when I found my passion for jewelry design.

During this time, I would have a recurring dream that I think was my psyche trying to protect me – I still have it sometimes. The dream is this: my mother didn't die, but she ran away from and abandoned her life because she was ashamed of it.

That idea always felt sad because everyone only has this time and space to make the best of what they have. Around this time, I started learning more about personal growth, trauma healing, and the law of attraction. That's when I realized how powerful mindset was in shaping one's beliefs about themselves and their situation. And how those beliefs shape their reality.

When I graduated from university, I decided that it was time. Instead of building someone else's dream, I would build my own, and I've never looked back. That's when I started my first business (a jewelry company).

Following your dreams and living a creative life is not the easiest path, but it's the MOST fulfilling.

Even though it took a little time to figure it out, I used the GIFT of my creativity and my outside-of-the-box thinking to live an amazing life this far. To this day, I've founded four companies, found the love of my life, and currently teach other creative types to follow their dreams and turn them into reality.

Most importantly, I spend a lot of time doing things that make me feel alive, creative, passionate, and on purpose. I'm doing what I'm meant to do because I know there are no guarantees that I'll be here tomorrow.

If you're reading this, I want to remind you that you can do anything you want, regardless of your circumstances or situation. Don't wait another day to do "the thing" that's calling to you, whether starting a business, finding true love, being of service, taking a dream vacation, or building a passion project. Find a way.

If you align your creative gifts with your passion, anything is possible.

You're not too old or too young. You can find the resources. Don't put your dreams on hold because tomorrow may not come.

Tracy Matthews

Valerie Venables

Every storm of life has a beginning, and every storm has an ending. Storms can be bittersweet. This means difficult roads often lead to beautiful destinations.

At fifteen, I was dating a boy who, five years later, became my husband. We entered our marriage full of hopes and dreams. Our future was bright. We talked about a family. Three years later, we were excited to have a daughter. Then, our family was perfect with the arrival of our son. Seven years into marriage, I was so happy. I loved being a wife, and I loved being a mother. I had a perfect family and a good marriage. My husband and I loved each other. Life was good. Unknown to me, I was heading towards a shipwreck that would be the worst storm of my life. Two weeks before my son's first birthday, my husband left carrying a suitcase with a few belongings. He said he loved us and walked out the front door. I stood at the top of the entrance stairs, numb and in shock.

What just happened? Three months earlier, he had been acting strange. Amazing what guilt does. I thought he was stressed out about work. Our home was peaceful. The next day, things got even worse. I received a troubling phone call. A friend told me my husband was having an affair with a woman I thought was a friend. My heart was broken. My spirit was crushed. Being a child of divorce, I made a vow my children would never experience a broken home. But a good marriage takes two committed partners. Now, at twenty-seven, I was a single mom. Not a place I wanted to be. I was scared and had no idea about my future. I could not eat or sleep, and I lost a lot of weight. I was in the hospital for five days. Everyone was concerned.

Days passed into weeks, months, and then years. I tried to be strong to keep life as normal as I could. What's normal anyway? During the day, I was busy with the children. Evening routines remained the same: bath time, storytime, prayers, cuddles, and bedtime. After the children fell asleep, the house became so quiet. It felt like it was dead. I listened to the clock's ticking; it did not comfort my loneliness. I had many questions: what did I do wrong? My husband had many outdoor toys and enjoyed many activities with his friends. He had a lot of freedom. I watched the clock frantically, waiting for ten o'clock so I could go to bed and put the day behind me.

Remember, "When Life Gives You, Lemons Make Lemonade".

My mind was a battleground, and I was losing the war. How could a woman have an affair with a married man, especially a so-called friend? This question haunted me for a long time. I had a problem trusting women for years. Snuggled in bed, I would turn my lamp off. The room was dark now, with a bit of light shining through the blinds from the bright moon outside. I tried to pray, but I must be honest; my prayers were very feeble. It was hard to know what to pray. God seemed so far away. The Bible talks about faith the size of a mustard seed. So, with mustard-size faith, I prayed for peace and rest. Night after night, the darkness was my enemy. I dreaded those long, lonely nights.

Morning always came too early. Rays of sunshine dawned outside and shone brightly into my bedroom. It felt like I had just fallen asleep. I yearned for the darkness. Sounds of pitter-patter of little feet came from the hallway. The house was coming alive. The children ran into my bedroom, jumped on the bed, dove under the covers, and snuggled beside me.

Their warm bodies were so comforting. They wanted to play, and I just wanted to sleep. I was exhausted. We played, then got up for breakfast. While sipping on my warm cup of coffee, thoughts raced through my head. It seemed like I was at the starting line of an Olympic marathon.

How was I going to get to the finish line? After breakfast, daily routines began, and then I'd drive my daughter to play school. Back home, chores began like yesterday and the days before.

I embraced these days with little strength, energy, or confidence. A mother's duty is a labor of love, and I loved being a mom. At noon, I picked my daughter up, and we came home for lunch. After lunch, time was set aside for the children—Storytime, pool time, walks, or visiting. My children were a gift from the Lord. They were my world! They brought so much joy and gave my life purpose. I believed I would be single for the rest of my life. I was shy, and the thought of dating was scary. I was willing to be single and lonely for the rest of my life. I was not going to sacrifice my children for my happiness. I told my mom, "If I ever remarry, that person has to love the children the same way I do." I thought that was impossible.

I was a Christian and was amazed when the Lord allowed us a second chance to be a family. This time, my husband would be God's choice. This man was respectful, kind, and had a soft heart towards the Lord. He was tall, dark, and handsome. He had an amazing sense of humour. When he entered a room, it lit up. His name was David, the same name as my ex-husband, which made things awkward for me. I liked the name, David. It was my son's middle name, meaning "beloved of God." The best thing about this man was he loved my children. All his attributes made me feel extremely comfortable.

He was the type of man most women would dream of. I was feeling blessed. I remember telling my mom, "Mom, he makes me laugh, and it feels so good." I had not laughed in a long time. It was his personality that won my heart.

After two weeks of dating and spending time with the children, Dave asked me to marry him. I said, "No." He asked two more times. Each time, I said, "No". The third time, he cried. I was sad that I hurt him. That was not my intention. He said, "I will never ask you again. I will wait until you're ready. Just let me know." I tried to explain that he was not the problem. I was the problem. I had baggage I had to deal with. Three years later, I was ready to trust again and commit.

We talked and set our wedding date for May 28th, 1980. Plans were set in motion for a small, intimate garden wedding with family and a few close friends, and the big day arrived. It was a beautiful, sunny day. The garden was in full bloom with an array of beautiful colors and sweet fragrances. Our guests had arrived and were waiting for us. The children were excited even before we got to the garden. Everything was perfect. In front of our guests, David and I said our wedding vows, making a lifetime commitment to each other. The next day, we left for a little honeymoon in Victoria. We knew God was writing our love story. It is truly amazing how one can find love when least expecting it.

Marriage Box...

People often get married believing a myth that marriage is a beautiful box full of all the things they have longed for: companionship, intimacy, friendship, etc... The truth is that marriage, at the start, is an empty box; you must put something in before you can take anything out. There is no love in marriage; love is in people, and people put love in marriage. There is no romance in marriage, and you must introduce it into your marriage. A couple must learn the art and the habit of giving, loving, serving, and praising one another. This keeps the marriage box full. If you take out more than you put in, the box will be empty.

Dave and I were unaware that God had big plans for our future. He planned to create a beautiful family and prepare us as a couple for ministry. Years after we moved to Kamloops, Dave became the Worship Pastor of our church. We went through some painful trials to prepare us for ministry. It was a walk of faith, one step at a time. Ecclesiastes 4:12: "A three-strand cord is not easily broken." In every trial, God was the third strand that held us together. He was our source of peace and our strength. He helped us overcome every obstacle and trial. Romas 8:28: "In all things God works things for the good of those who love him, who have been called according to his purpose."

On May 28th, 2020, we celebrated our 40th wedding anniversary. It seems like our journey began yesterday and feels like forever, all simultaneously. We have weathered many storms and have learned to ride the waves of the high seas. It has been a life full of joy, laughter, and tears all rolled up together. Retirement plans were in our future, and we looked forward to growing old together. Our best days were ahead of us. We had come a long way, yet it felt like we were just beginning. We enjoyed being together, and our love was stronger than ever. Our eyes were fixed on the Lord. Ministry never ends; it just changes. We felt that our ministry would be outside the church's walls. Just like Jesus, we would go to the lost. Little did we know another shipwreck was around the corner. This would be even worse than my divorce.

Shortly after our 40th anniversary, my husband passed away suddenly from cancer, and I became a widow. I lost my husband, my best friend, my companion, my provider, my protector, and my lover. God had given Dave forty-four years of grace as he had the same cancer at twenty-one. After that, Dave embraced every day as a gift and lived it like his last. My husband lived well and touched many people, both young and old. His legacy lives on in the hearts of all those he touched over the years. Here, I stood in front of another crossroad. The process of grief is a long, difficult road. This was an unexpected season for me. I was older than my husband, so I never thought I'd be the partner left behind. Now Dave is in heaven with the King of Kings, the one he loved the most. He is with our two babies that we lost years ago. Dave is one more treasure in heaven. God promises us that we will be reconciled with our loved ones in glory. I stand on that promise. The Lord said he would be the husband to the widower. My faith is strong, and I have peace knowing that I will see my husband again someday. Oh, another storm behind me. Some days are harder than others, but I am good. Almost three years now, and I still miss my husband every day. I have no idea what my future holds, but I do know who holds my future. Whatever storm you are going through, know there will be an ending and a new beginning. Once again, I choose to make lemonade. Cheers...

Remember, *"When Life Gives You, Lemons Make Lemonade".*

Valerie Venables

Yoav Shimoni

The Murder of my grandmother during the October 7th Terror Attacks was broadcasted to me and my whole family through my grandmother's Facebook page.

If I could leave you with one piece of advice about resilience, it would be to embrace and appreciate the people you love and who love you.

It was the night between the 6th and the 7th of October, and I was in Toronto, preparing for an upcoming flight to British Columbia in the morning as the news of missiles hitting Israel started to come out. I messaged my friends and family to ensure their safety. After everyone's safety was confirmed, and my mom even mentioned my grandmother's concern for them in Tel Aviv above her safety, my sister mentioned that my grandmother posted something odd on Facebook.

I then opened Facebook and witnessed the video of my grandmother's murder by several terrorists who were standing above her with guns, yelling in Arabic as she was bleeding to death on the floor of her living room. At first, I was in shock. I was full of confusion and did not want to believe what I witnessed was real. I tried calling my parents. On the rare occasion that my father picked up, all I could hear was my mother's screams in the background as she tried contacting other people in the kibbutz to get more information and alert them. After that, I could not sleep the entire night for the next few days on my travels. That time was full of concussion, fear, and shock.

For several hours after my family and I saw the video, there wasn't even an official confirmation that terrorists had infiltrated Israel. The feeling of uncertainty only compounded with time, as it took over a month to receive DNA confirmation (it took so long because the house with my grandmother in it was burnt by the terrorists after her murder) and begin the mourning period.

The video kept playing in my head, and "what if" thoughts kept rising. Especially as my entire family and I stayed at my grandmother's house for Rosh Hashana only a week before the attacks. After getting to British Columbia, I was fortunate to stay with my partner, who helped me cope.

Just her presence and the knowledge that I was not alone at this time was more than I could ask for.

Her father also flew over to help distract me and cope with the events. I also began meeting with a therapist to help come up with healthy ways to cope. Now, looking back, I believe I hindered my therapy's effectiveness by accepting many interviews where I shared my story without having the chance to truly process what happened or even mourn for my grandmother.

Which, in turn, made the therapy sessions feel repetitive and removed my ability to open up emotionally. I then began to focus on work and distance myself from social media. That helped a lot, but I think the thing that helped me cope the most was returning to Israel to attend my grandmother's funeral as soon as they identified the body. This allowed me to be with my family at this time. Mourn with them, and not only them but everyone in Israel. I could see the remains of my grandmother's house and the Kibbutz. This was a difficult experience, but it allowed me to get closure by seeing it with my own eyes. The ability to be in Israel during the war, seeing what the situation is really like on the ground, and not through a tilted media lens, helped relieve a lot of anxieties.

Due to the general spirit caused by the war and most people having someone who died, was kidnapped, or is currently serving, it felt like there was no option but to be resilient.

If I could leave you with one piece of advice about resilience, it would be to embrace and appreciate the people you love and who love you.

Yoav Shimoni

Conclusion

In the heart of every individual lies an innate resilience, a strength that we are all born with. While some may need to draw upon this resilience more frequently than others, it is a universal trait embedded within us. Life doesn't come with a manual, especially during challenging times. The narratives of resilience shared within these pages illuminate that even in the darkest moments, there is a guiding light, assuring you that you will emerge triumphant.

These compelling stories serve as a testament to the human spirit, offering tangible proof that hard times are not insurmountable obstacles. They showcase the resilience inherent in us all and serve as a source of inspiration, providing a roadmap for navigating your own difficult moments. Whether you find strength today or in the face of a future challenge, these stories are here to guide you.

If the stories within this book, our podcast, our website, or any other platform where you encounter us leave you feeling empowered and inspired, we invite you to share our community. Our space is one of safety and healing, created to be a sanctuary for those in need. Whether you seek solace in the stories of others or wish to share your resilience journey, we are here for you.

By sharing your story on theglobalresilienceproject.com, you contribute to The Global Resilience Project, potentially paving the way for more impactful books that echo the strength found in collective resilience. Tune in to our podcast, Radical Resilience, available on your favorite podcast player, for more stories that remind you of the indomitable human spirit.

It's important to acknowledge that it's okay not to be OK. In those moments, remember that brighter days lie ahead, and within you resides an unyielding resilience.

You will bounce forward. You are resilient.

Navigating Grief Framework

This framework was created by the founder of The Global Resilience Project, Blair Kaplan Venables, to help you navigate grief.

The Navigating Grief Framework can serve as a structured path to healing while acknowledging the unique pressures high performers may face. You can follow this process on your own, or you can work with our team to help you. Grief isn't linear, and neither is your healing, so follow this framework in whatever order your choose.

G - Grounding in the Present

1. **Mindfulness:** Encourage the practice of mindfulness to stay anchored in the current moment, which can help manage overwhelming emotions.

2. **Routine:** Maintain a simple daily routine to provide structure and a sense of normalcy amidst the chaos of grief.

3. **Daily Gratitude Practice**

R - Resilience muscle rituals and Routines

1. **Acknowledge Feelings:** Recognize and accept the range of emotions that come with grief, understanding that they are a natural and necessary part of the healing process.

2. **Express Emotions:** Find healthy outlets for emotional expression, such as journaling, art, or talking with a trusted confidant.

I - Introspection for Understanding

1. **Reflect on Loss:** Allocate time to reflect on the loss and its impact on life, acknowledging both the pain and the cherished memories.

2. **Personal Values:** Reconnect with personal values and beliefs that may provide comfort or a sense of purpose during this time.

E - Engagement with Support Systems

1. **Community:** Actively seek and engage with supportive communities, whether friends, family, support groups, or professional counselors.

2. **Helping Others:** Consider ways to help others, which can create feelings of purpose and connection and can be therapeutic in managing one's grief.

F - Forward Movement

1. **Set Realistic Goals:** Establish small, manageable goals to foster a sense of progress and accomplishment.

2. **Adaptation:** Recognize and adapt to the 'new normal,' understanding that moving forward doesn't mean forgetting but finding a way to carry the memory of the lost one into the future.

3. **Find a new meaning:** Explore new activities, hobbies, or causes that can bring a renewed sense of meaning and joy into your life. Sometimes, building new connections or discovering new passions can help in the healing process.

The Navigating Grief Framework is meant to be flexible, recognizing that each individual's journey through grief is personal and can vary widely in experience and duration.

Acknowledgements

In the journey of bringing this book to life, profound gratitude is owed to a group of exceptional individuals, each of whom has played an indispensable role in weaving together the tapestry of stories contained within these pages.

Catherine Nikkel, our editor, whose discerning eye and unyielding dedication to excellence have enhanced the quality of our work and guided us with wisdom and insight through every chapter. Your expertise and passion for storytelling have been the beacon that led us to the completion of this project.

Patrica Saville, our Project Manager, deserves our heartfelt thanks for her impeccable organization and steadfast support. Your ability to navigate the complexities of this project, ensuring that every deadline was met and every detail accounted for, has been nothing short of remarkable. Your leadership has been a cornerstone of our success. You have kept my brain organized, and I'm lucky to have you on the team.

Ruth Barrow, our graphic designer, whose artistic talent has brought visual life to our words, created a beautiful book that is a pleasure to behold. Your creativity and dedication to capturing the essence of our stories in every design element have added immeasurable value to this work.

To my husband, Shayne Venables, your unwavering support and encouragement have been my rock. Your belief in my vision, even in moments of doubt, has been a source of strength and inspiration. Thank you for being my partner in every sense of the word through this project and in life.

Our cats, Molly (Alana's cat), Frey, and Duffy (my cats), have been silent companions whose presence has added comfort and joy to many working sessions. Your unassuming companionship and quirky antics have often been the light-hearted relief needed during the intensity of creation.

To Zoloft, thank you for helping to keep the chemicals in my brain balanced and helping me manage my depression and PMDD.

To the strangers on the Internet, thank you for your ongoing support and encouragement with this project. The Global Resilience Project is a labour of love, and you are always there to remind us why we do this work.

Lastly, to the coauthors who entrusted us with their stories of resilience, your courage and openness have been the soul of this book. Your experiences and insights have made this work not just a collection of stories but a beacon of hope and inspiration for others.

To each of you, I extend my deepest gratitude. This book is a reflection of mine and Alana's vision and testament to the collective effort, talent, and spirit of all who contributed to its creation. Thank you for being part of this journey.

Love Blair

Connect
with us

Connect with The Global Resilience Project

THE GLOBAL RESILIENCE
PROJECT'S WEBSITE:

theglobalresilienceproject.com

SUBMIT YOUR STORY:

theglobalresilienceproject.com/submit

EMAIL US:
info@theglobalresilienceproject.com

READ MORE STORIES OF RESILIENCE:
theglobalresilienceproject.com/stories-of-resilience

MERCHANDISE:
theglobalresilienceproject.com/shop

RADICAL RESILIENCE PODCAST:
theglobalresilienceproject.com/radical-resilience

INSTAGRAM: @globalresiliencecommunity

FACEBOOK: @globalresiliencecommunity

TIKTOK: @griefygals

Connect with our Founder, Blair Kaplan Venables:

EMAIL: blair@blairkaplan.ca
WEBSITE: www.blairkaplan.ca

@BLAIRFROMBLAIRLAND
BLAIRDKAPLAN
FACEBOOK.COM/BLAIR.KAPLAN
FACEBOOK.COMBLAIRKAPLANCOMMUNICATIONS

CHECK OUT BLAIR
AND THE GLOBAL
RESILIENCE PROJECT
IN FORBES
+ OTHER FUN LINKS

linktr.ee/
blairkaplanvenables

Additional Resources and Support

For bulk sales of RESILIENT A.F.: Stories of Resilience contact Blair Kaplan Venables, Founder of The Global Resilience Project: **blair@blairkaplan.ca.**

To purchase our first book, The Global Resilience Project, head to **Amazon.com** (or the Amazon available to you in your region).

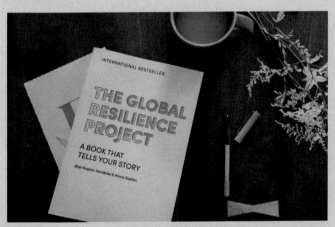

To hire Blair Kaplan Venables for grief and resilience support or to book her as a speaker at your next event or to be a guest on your podcast, radio or television show, email: **blair@blairkaplan.ca.**

Blair is also available for opportunities to feature her writing in your publication.

Your
Thoughts

Made in the USA
Las Vegas, NV
03 September 2024

94699670R00088